CHARGES

(The Supplicants)

THE GERMAN LIST

CHARGES
(The Supplicants)

ELFRIEDE JELINEK

TRANSLATED BY GITTA HONEGGER

LONDON NEW YORK CALCUTTA

This publication was supported by a grant from the Austrian Federal
Ministry for Education, Arts and Culture, and the Goethe-Institut India.

Seagull Books, 2016

Elfriede Jelinek, DIE SCHUTZBEFOHLENEN

© Elfriede Jelinek, 2013

Performing rights: Rowohlt Theater Verlag, Reinbek

Published by permission of Rowohlt Verlag GmbH, Reinbek.

Translation © Gitta Honegger, 2016

ISBN 978 0 8574 2 330 6

British Library Cataloguing-in-Publication Data
A catalogue record for this book is available from the British Library.

Typeset by Seagull Books, Calcutta, India
Printed and bound by Maple Press, York, Pennsylvania, USA

CONTENTS

A group of asylum seekers from Central Asia and the Middle East leave a large holding facility in a small town on the outskirts of the capital city. To draw attention to their plight, they march into the city's beautiful, historic center and set up camp without permission of the municipal authorities in the small park in front of a well-known church. A couple of weeks later some of the refugees move inside the church. The Interior Ministry and the media get involved. The refugees go on a hunger strike. There are public demonstrations in support of the undocumented migrants. They trigger impassioned public arguments for and against granting asylum to the people who escaped life-threatening situations and mourn the extinction of their families. One month after the arrival of the migrants the police clear the park of the campers. Others remain in the church for ten more weeks, while politicians either scramble or attack each other trying to finesse a way out of the embarrassing situation. The asylum seekers are finally transferred to a nearby monastery, a secluded temporary refuge to keep them out of public sight. Not long before the refugees arrived in the city, a world-famous opera singer and the daughter of a former powerful politician, both from privileged backgrounds in another country, had been awarded citizenship with the help of a powerful industrialist who also founded a new populist political party which won a number of seats in parliament at around the same time. Sadly, this story of precarity and privilege is happening around the world. Countries, victims, celebrities and moneyed power brokers are exchangeable.

As usual, Elfriede Jelinek's performance text was triggered by a specific event that began in Vienna in November 2012, as outlined in the above narrative.

The actual asylum seekers were from Afghanistan and Pakistan. They occupied the Votiv-*Kirche* on Vienna's splendid Ringstrasse that encircles the historic core of the city. The prominent singer stands for Anna Netrebko, the Russian star of the Salzburg Festival and leading opera houses worldwide. The other Russian woman is Tatyana Yumesheva the daughter of the first free-market president of the newly created Russian Soviet Federative Republic, Boris Yeltsin. The entrepreneur refers to Austrian-Canadian Frank Stronach, who strategized Yumesheva's naturalization as an Austrian citizen. For this he won the support of the *Sberbank of Russia* to finance the acquisition of an Opel plant in Vienna. The deal was eventually vetoed by General Motors, the American owner of the Opel corporation.

The "real life" personalities are referred to by the choral speakers in archetypical terms, such as the singer, the industrialist turned politician, the daughter of a former Russian president. They never enter as stage characters, though they are the driving forces, the plotters, as it were, of the "plot" of the "drama" emerging from the choral passages. Accordingly, the actual places of events are referred to in general terms: a church, a monastery, a lake, a city famous for its international summer festival. This indicates that the urgent issues raised by the local event have universal relevance.

In Jelinek's characteristic dramaturgical approach the text features no designated speakers and at first suggests a Chorus. Reading the text and its musical undertones out loud will reveal that the voices of the speakers change, even in the middle of a sentence. Punctuations in the long run-on sentences function as musical notations rather than in accordance with grammatical rules. The rhythm often suggests the breathless anguish, confusion and hurry of the refugees and the writer's own deeply conflicted response to the situation. Jelinek's method allows directors, dramaturgs and actors to discover individual characters / speakers or the representative voice of a social group a given text passage or sentence represents. Referring to some of her defining directors (as well as translators) as "co-authors," she has also given her directors the freedom to "carve out" their text. She has given me as her authorized translator the freedom to change her long chain of intricate word-games into equivalent American-English idioms and colloquialisms.[1]

Jelinek characteristically interweaves texts from the Western canon with trivia from media and social networks into immediate concerns. Aeschylus's *The Supplicants* introduces the motif of daughters (the fifty daughters of Danaus) fleeing from their homeland (to avoid forced

---

1 For a detailed discussion of Jelinek's dramaturgy see Introduction in Elfriede Jelinek, *Rechnitz and The Merchant's Contracts* (Gitta Honegger trans. and introd.) (Calcutta: Seagull Books, 2015), pp. 1–62.

marriages), and echoes the heightened language of Greek tragedy.

Martin Heidegger's tracking of word roots and their transformations in his philosophical investigations of origin and meaning serves as a target of mockery that exposes the dangerous nativism and populism deeply embedded in his thinking and convoluted language. T. S. Eliot's poem *The Hollow Men* provides the leitmotif of hollowness—the literal, physical hollowness of the emaciated victims and perpetrators' mental/spiritual hollowness. Nietzsche's Zarathustra adds his mocking worldview.

Jelinek had already mulled over writing a text in response to the refugees' drama while it was still unraveling in Vienna at that time, when one of her favorite directors, Nicolas Stemann inquired whether she would be interested in contributing a short text for his *Commune of Truth. Reality Machine* project. He was already in the process of devising this performance with his company for the Vienna Festival 2013. Jelinek considered this the perfect opportunity to draw renewed attention to the refugees' predicament. In his signature method of directing Jelinek's plays (most prominently *The Merchant's Contracts*) Stemann usually requested additional topical material from Elfriede Jelinek that applied specifically to the cities and international festivals where his productions toured. Frequently, when Jelinek is asked to provide a text for a specific occasion, her contribution develops into an autonomous performance text, too long and too compact and too tightly woven to extract a few passages for just another sketch in a collaboratively devised hi-tech spectacle of improvisations on the daily news in the framework of original soundtracks and video clips of the daily news interspersed with songs appropriated from both popular culture and classical music.

Although the text had lost its immediate site-specific context, its primary concerns and circumstances—streams of displaced people, xenophobia, political corruption and favoritism are an urgent global concern. Streams of refugees from Africa continue to try to reach Europe in ramshackle overcrowded boats. If they survive the precarious crossing, they first land on the Italian island of Lampedusa. According to European Union law, undocumented refugees must stay in the country of their first arrival until their asylum request is either granted or denied. However, the Italian Government frequently offers them (short-term) tourist visas in order to pass on the overflow to other European countries. For many Germany is a desired destination. At one point, 80 of around 300 African refugees found accommodation in Hamburg's St. Paul Lutheran Church. The presence of these refugees inspired a staged reading of *Charges* in the church, co-sponsored by its pastor Sieghard Wilm, and Joachim Lux, the artistic director of Hamburg's Thalia Theatre. The presentation included the refugees and actors from the theatre's resident company. At the time of the reading in September 2013, the refugees' fate was not yet decided. The following year, in May 2014, a full production of the play, now directed by Nicolas Stemann, premiered at the quadrennial Theatre of the

World Festival (Theater der Welt) in Mannheim. It was co-produced by the Festival and the Thalia Theatre and included local refugees along naturalized or first-generation German professional actors and some stalwart Jelinek performers from the Thalia ensemble. *Charges* was the 'keynote' production introducing the Festival's focus on cultural diversity and precarity at a time when political crises, religious conflicts and local wars further intensified the tragedies of migrants and refugees around the world. As I am writing this preface (April 2015), reports of the drowning of refugees on their way to Lampedusa or the Greek Islands continue to make news on a nearly daily basis. At the same time, the plight of unaccompanied children crossing from Mexico to the United States was gaining increasing attention in the media. Furthermore, the explosive conditions in Gaza, Syria, the Ukraine, Iraq and ongoing conflicts around the world continue to turn millions of people into migrants and refugees.

As with her previous play *The Merchant's Contracts* which dealt with the ongoing global economic crisis, Jelinek continued to add sequels to the main text of *Charges* titled *Coda* and *Appendix*. 'Coda' was written in response to the many reports of the drowning or bare survival of African refugees packed by irresponsible smugglers into overcrowded, ramshackle boats. The speakers draw from the countless media reports and images of such tragedies. One image gone viral showed a smuggler in green swim trunks pushing the crowded boat into the water and then swimming back to the shore. The irony was not lost on Jelinek. She refers to him in the *Coda* as the 'dolphin man'. In her signature style Jelinek also inserts herself into the text. The occasional interjections of the author's voice suggest a woman surrounded by television screens, smartphones, newspapers and magazines in dialog with the unfolding events. Such personal interjections become more frequent and intense in the second addendum *Appendix*. As she clarifies the title with characteristic self-deprecating irony, it should indicate that the piece is not a direct continuation of the preceding texts but rather attached to them like the anatomical appendix—a small thin extension without a specific function of a long continuous tube.² Though not indicated in a stage direction, the scenario emerging from the text's musical composition suggests the author obsessively following the unstoppable refugee crisis, struggling to come to terms with the absurdity of her own position: the writer as a solitary but intensely engaged observer, driven by the need to intervene in the events as they happen. Though fully aware of the futility of any such attempt Jelinek compulsively tries to catch up with them. Therefore her performance texts cannot reach a closure. They remain open to history in action. Needless to say, this presents enormous challenges to the stage director— in this case her frequent collaborator Nicolas Stemann— and to the translator. In order to preserve the dynamic of the evolving texts they are published and introduced here in the chronological order of their development. A series of conversations with Elfriede Jelinek, who has not

---

2 Jelinek in a conversation with Honegger in Munich (January 2016).

granted a personal interview in over ten years, concludes the ongoing work on this publication in tandem with the close observation of the production process for the texts' word premiere.

CHARGES
(The Supplicants)

We are alive. We are alive. The main thing is we live and it hardly is more than that after leaving the sacred homeland. No one looks down with mercy at our train, but everyone looks down on us. We fled, not convicted by any court in the world, convicted by all, there and here. All things knowable about our lives are gone, choked beneath a layer of appearances, nothing is an object of knowledge anymore, there is no more. No more need to try to grasp anything. We try to read foreign laws. They tell us nothing, we find out nothing. We are summoned but not seen, we must appear here, then there; but which land that's lovelier than this—and we don't know of any—, which land can we set foot on? None. We stand around unsettled. We are sent away again. We lie down on the cold church floor. We get up again. We don't eat. We should eat, at least drink something again. We have some branches here, for peace, from the oil palm, no, we tore them off the olive tree, and this here too, all filled with writing; we have nothing else, whom may we hand this, this pile, we filled two tons of paper with our writing, we had help with that, of course, now we hold it up suppliantly, all that paper, no, we don't have papers, only paper, to whom may we give it? You? Please, here it is, but if you do nothing with it, we have to make another copy, print it all again, surely you are aware of that? Oh, you celestial ones above, devoutly we clasp our hands, yes, we mean you, look down, we are praying to you, yes you, who surely own the city and the land and the Danube's glistening waters and even more surely you, the harsh punishers in the bureaucracy: you tell us this and you tell us that, and there is nothing we can do right, but you are not right and just either, you angels, plus you, dear father in heaven. What could we do against you?, you can do anything, there is nothing you cannot do. You there, can you tell us please, who, what God lives here and is in charge, here in this church we know who, but maybe there are others, some other place, there is a president, a lady chancellor, a minister, okay, and of course there are also those punishing ones we noticed, not down in Hades, they are right next door, you, whoever, you, whoever you are, you, you, Jesus, Messiah, Messi, doesn't matter, who protects the house, the family line, you did not admit us, we came on our own, to your church, a train of supplicants, please help us, God, please help us, we set foot on your shore, our foot also stepped on quite different shores, when it was lucky, but how will it go from here? The sea almost destroyed us, the mountains almost destroyed us, now we are in the church, tomorrow we will be in the monastery, thanks to our Lord God, thanks to our Mr. President, they were called upon, they heeded the call, but where will we be the day after tomorrow and after that? Where will a bed be denied to us, where will we prevail, where will they kick us out again, where will we be able to bury our own bones, that is to say, who will do all that, who will do that for us? Who will make sure that we will also be seen as *beings*, and without disgust? Those chased away from the brook's banks, the ocean's shore, the forest's brush, mourning the lost homeland, bewildered by their ancient mothers' wrath, those are the ones you are seeing here, no one claims his descent from anyone here, little good would it do him here, and why are they angry with us here too? We don't understand. We have long been acquainted with pain, yes, but what have we done here that you keep us in fear, fear everywhere, fear of my people, whom I left, fear that I must go back again, yet still more fear of you, that I am forced to stay, that I cannot stay, and on this you will surely agree with me: If you are fear-filled everywhere, you will say, why did you come here? To have new fears so soon again? But now it is the local barbarians' language, speech we do not know; is it always like this in a different place, among foreign people, what will happen now? What could possibly happen? We call out to you suppliantly in this language we do not know and cannot speak, which you are in perfect control of, like of yourself, except when you are standing on a railway platform and see us coming, please try to experience just some of the things you can never know! Please!

Look at us, Sir, yes, you!, as supplicants we turn to you, someone conceived us, someone gave birth to us, we can understand that you want to check that, but you will not be able to. Wherever there is a somewhere else, we don't know anything, for whatever there is might be something else and always elsewhere anyway and whatever there is for us to recognize is Nothing. They sent us videos, to my family, when I still had one, they are dead now, all of them, dead, not one single one left there, my old horizon no longer a given, that's now a given, they are all gone, except myself, I am still here and what do they do with me? The horizon turns into nothing, it ends at the mountains, the sea is a hole, a gorge, no one there anymore, no one here, only me who is here and not there, but here, left with my memories, all dead, dead somewhere else, dead for sure, I am the last one, a hard lot, I loudly lament it, I drew the saddest lot. Here, look, two of my folks getting their heads cut off, a few relatives were still left after that, they shot it with the smart phone as long as there still was time, now that's no longer the case, they are no more, now there is only me, but this hard to unravel lot—for why are people doing that?—won't let me stay here, look here, that is me cutting up the jeans given to me, the donated sweater, I cut up the donated backpack right away, I must be crazy, those things belong to me now, after all!, I let myself be swept away by invisible waves, but does it do me any good? It doesn't. Two of my cousins beheaded, I beseech you, I know, you would not do that to me, you could never do that, but don't my two cousins speak for me? With their cut throats, their heads off? Doesn't it count in my favor, that I experienced such horror, don't you want us?, yes, you! Us, a dark, sun-raised group, we then turned around, but: where to? To other peoples, blooming on the night-side of the world, bombing the daylight out of the world, booming at the world's end. Everything in the earth's night, in the end's night, night everywhere where we are not, but should go and also want to, we, strangers in the night, is there a Mr. President, of one nation, under God, an all-accepting one? No, there isn't. There is no one all-accepting. There might be someone to sooner accept all the universe than us, nothing, no one will accept us. It is unheard of! And unheard is what we are.

We will remember you in angry speeches, but you won't care, we know that, for our being here will not be legal, and that is your favorite world, legal, legal, not legal your being here, no matter the testimony we give, the births, the care our women give, no matter how we break our backs for you, you couldn't care less, you turned your backs on us, despite our supplications, you turned your backs on us, we scratched them, it didn't help ours, still, we implore, we supplicate, we implore you up there, hello, if you don't want us, we'll still stay with you, as your charges, on the already discussed grounds no one lets us stand on. And even the decision as to the direction of our relocation, our retreat, which we don't even request, which you require, the return, no matter in what direction, out, just out of here, is denied to us. This paper, this signed paper orders our return into the bombed, the bummed-out land, where we came from: Where were you last? You must file your request there! This is what you want from us, you do want something after all! The head, they cut the heads off my two cousins, there is no one to testify, there is one thing to testify: the camera, no one, no place without it nowadays, hanging everywhere, attached to anything, everything can be proven on the spot, here you can see it, see the proof, in this video, how two men are getting their heads cut off, isn't that horrifying? You don't believe it, but you can see it, you see it right there, my family has the video, but they don't exist anymore, the family, they are all dead now, only the video is left, no one feels any shame about it, only you are ashamed for me, your imagination can't deal with that, there is no dealing with you, you are the one dealing out, dealing everyone out, that is the deal, get them out of here, people conceived and born, chasing them away, you do that well. And chopping off heads, which is nothing compared to all the ways of suffering, which have gone on forever and everywhere and those methods took much longer, for obvious reasons. Only suffering lasts. No one gets worked up about that. It won't get anyone out of the woodwork. Father, mother, children murdered, but that's nothing. All our thoughts are focused on objects, sub-jects don't count, the dead don't count, they don't exist. We can't refer to the dead to make folks here convert our status. No, what they want is to divert us, (the 'them' into them), like rivers, streaming into a Nowhere they cannot flood, or an ocean they cross illegally, those streams, where they can no longer cut through or out, where they won't cut throats and we couldn't cut it either. Divert, deport, good riddance to them and nothing to ride on us. All dead, why should I, the last one, still be alive? You can't understand that. I don't understand it either. But if time, that three-parts-in-one, the tri-unity, if it also includes us, no, not God, not the trinity, they never were a unity, I am talking about the three tenses of time in one time which never united anything, which united us, as a group, which threw us together, a bunch of nobodies and nothings, have-nothings for sure, well then, if time, as I just said, I can't really say it, if time is this tri-unified whole of presentness, past-presentness and future, and if the thinker—hide-egg—something like that, I don't know him, but he thinks, the thinker, if he now added to the two modi, which have been proven to produce time, so then, if the thinker added to the two a third modus—but which?, which one?,—that would enable us to stay and thus be outside of time, so that we also can get out again, well, an additional modus, how come, there are already three, past, present and the future, whatever, if it were the way I said, actually, it wasn't me, it was that Heidegghead, but if I were to say it, if I could think that way, I don't know what this *that way* means, in any case, if we think of all ways of imagining that includes thinking—and you don't give a damn, uh, penny for our thoughts, which yield nothing, they don't make a killing—, so then, if this thinking, your thinking is also subject to time, then this third modus of the synthesis must shape, inform, enlighten the future, no future for the unenlightened, but nothing for the enlightened either, nothing for anyone, time then must make the future like a dress. And? And, now what? Will this land's bosses, the heads of states, who, unlike my cousins still have their heads attached to their bodies, will they, alerted by this fast urgent mission, that slow foreign mission, whatever, will they come in person to see us? They won't. We would tell the bosses in this land and the representatives of the bosses in this land and the representatives of the representatives of the bosses in this land, we would, we aren't allowed to, but we would, as it befits aliens, we would speak understandingly, understandably of our bloodguilt-free flight, we would be happy to tell anyone, it would not have to be a representative, we would do it, we promise; we tell everyone, we would tell anyone who would want to hear it, but no one does, not even a representative's representative wants to hear it, no one, but we would tell of our crimeless flight without guilt, which you always present as a flight from debts, thus the flight of the guilt-free-on-all-counts is what we would speak of, our voice will be free of

insolence, of falsehood, we will be calm, courteous, com-
posed, and understandable, understandably so, but you will
not understand, how could you, as you don't even want to
hear it, thus our voice will fall into a void, into weightless-
ness, our lot that weighs so heavily on us will suddenly be
weightless, because it will fall into Nothingness, into a vac-
uum, into the absolute Nothing, where it will hover, where
we will try to hang on, in the water, in the void, yes.
Through our unassuming eyes we will look at you softly and
ask for a blanket, for food; now look, your reps' representatives will say: Your eyes are not unassuming at all, even
though you say so they assume certain things—that you
deserve blankets, water and food, what will you think you
deserve tomorrow? Our wives, our children, our jobs, our
homes? What will you ask for tomorrow? Today you might
not ask for a lot, but tomorrow it will be a lot, we already
know, and that is why we are the deputies of deputies of
deputies, they all know it, everyone knows it, and now we
know too, even though we knew it before. We knew. What?
What are you saying? We are careful not to be bold or long-
winded or too detailed or dull, or too fast or too slow when
we talk. We must not be any of it, unfortunately, we don't
speak your language, where is the interpreter? where did he
go?, you promised us one, so where is he, where is the man
who tells us we should not talk too slowly or too fast. Who
says so? Doesn't matter, for creatures like us are all too odi-
ous to you, we can tell. That much is clear. You should give
in as we gave in when we went from the church to the
monastery, where it is warm and we will rot faster, decom-
pose more quickly, our selves scurrying away like mice. We

gave in and now we are gone, taken out of your sight, out of the public's eye, taken away, they told us, we did it: You must give in, they told us and after some time we did: You must give in, we were told, we are told all the time, told now too, you must give in, fugitive, foreign, in need, as you are here, you must give in just as you are, you must give in, there, you see, now you got it, you gave in; fugitive, foreign and needy, someone like that is not permitted to speak here, someone like that is not permitted to be here. For forward speech never befits the unfortunate. How unbecoming! How could we be coming, when we are always kept going? We will be reasonable and you will tell someone that you reasoned with us and we have finally been brought to reason, ready to move from the church to the monastery, which stands empty right now, they are already showing it on TV, they already talk about it on the radio, it will soon be in the papers, the church is also empty, but it stands, it stands its ground even better, every follower invested in his God should be able to enter, and we would stand in the way, we can understand that, as we have heavily invested in our God, who yields exclusively to the debt-free guiltless. Yes, and? What does that get us now? Have pity on us, before danger crushes us, please!, please!, please! No? That's what we thought. So there is your light-wingèd god hanging, standing everywhere, thousands of statues, gold, glitter, flush of colors, bling, bling, please, we say tentatively, maybe this one will help us, though he is not responsible for us, but that deputy of a deputy of a deputy of a God, whom you just hung there so we would hang here too, no, not for that, so there he hangs, poor fellow, didn't have much luck in his life either, whatever, to this light-winged eagle is where it gets us now, no, that doesn't nail it, this is not an eagle, the eagle is that little thing up there, above him, look, you can see it quite well from here, up there, so that's not an eagle you say, that's supposed to be a dove?, what can you expect from a dove? Just as little. Duh!, a dove, a female bird, a deputress?, debutrix, a lady rep of a lady rep of a lady rep, whatever, the lady is a bird, so she can fly and it is her I call upon in prayer, my call is a prayer, I have to call someone, okay, and then I call my lawyer, but right now I call out a prayer to that dove on the roof, imploring her, suppliantly, you, sun's first responding eye inside the triangle, eye of the sun, hitting the cathedral ceiling, you, yes, we mean you!, you heard right, we implore you of all godly things! There's no one else around. No reason to suddenly hit the ceiling mad with anger! Now the sh* *t got stuck in the ceiling fan, what can we do?

The fact that they are all dead now, the whole family, won't get you anywhere here. We sit here, we greet politely, we don't care whom, we don't care what God it is, they told us, we forgot, but civility dictates us to devoutly greet all the high powers in these pictures and that one out front, alone on his altar, *Grüß Gott*, "God bless" is what you say here or how shall I say it. We huddled in this sacred place like a flock of doves, but folks here only know this one dove up there on the roof, that one is too high up, there is no hawk that dove must fear, and we? We must fear everything and every-one. That's just the way it is. All fell victim to kindred foes. But who accepts such sacrifices? It would take a lot of gods to accept this many sacrificial victims! There is no one left, no one for all I care, not one of ours. They killed them all. I fled, by now the last, the very last of my big, beloved family, one resister killing another until only one side is left, supposedly that's our custom, our tradition, but that's only boasting. And still there are always more left of the ones than the others, especially the ones, the others they kill, but what will happen once no one is left? Well, we can't go through the whole sequence of imagining, you wouldn't be able to imagine it anyway, no one could, except if he had a video; the sequence of memories broken like my family, torn apart, murdered, and here, may I, as the last one, sit here at least? Just sit down? I don't even have to lie down. Or rather there? Would you rather have me sit there?, then I will! I have no position here, so you could easily point me to an opening, a place I may settle down. The freedom to settle is the law here, but not for us. It does not include the dead either, and except for myself everyone is dead, all dead. So you can easily count me among them. I can already hear you laugh, you know that the dead no longer ask for anything, but I am still asking, turned to you suppliantly, some clothes, a bit of food, water, a place. We even have proof that all others are dead, no, no one else will come, don't you worry!, no one except us, no one except us will bother you, we have videos, the murderers have modern equipment for everything. We are not modern, but the murderers are, they are modern and not modern at the same time, they are everything, for murderers are everything and they can do anything. We are in possession of knowledge, but who is interested in that, who cares about knowledge, it's not interesting, nothing that cannot be shown is interesting. Not to us either. Look, now you can see it too: Resistance against us appears on the horizon. We hide in churches, in monasteries, but we are not supposed to stay or it wouldn't be a hideout. This church is an open hiding place, TV was already here, they bring everything to light, the lights they are bringing themselves. There is someone lying right here, another one over there, doomed forever for being foreign. He won't be the only one. He won't be the last one left, the one to leave alive, but he won't be allowed to live here either, says the opposition whose headlines are blinding us, he better dim them. Even if someone drove toward him on the highway, in the opposite direction, a "ghost-driver," as they call it here, he mustn't try to get out of your way, and he mustn't try to get around us either, he must back away from us. Backing away from a ghost driver is difficult. Only getting around him works sometimes. No. Sure! It doesn't work. They all back off from us, a swarm of barbarians. All people, no matter were they live, back away inadvertently from foreign clothes and veils, from us swarming savages, their reflex reaction to make room for random action. That is what they bring in for help these days. It would have been simpler to help us, it would even be simpler not to help us, but so be it. You are backing off, well then, randomness take over, do as you wish! We have no veils to suit your customs or taste, we are simply veiled, like everyone else, but we know, even if we were to look like you: you would spot us, you would recognize us among thousands, you would spot us anywhere, you would know we don't belong here.

Appeal is no longer possible, not even with reference to the dead, no need to appear. Harmonious togetherness is requested, no, not from the dead, they are gone, from us, because we are supposed to contribute to the common prosperity. How does that work? What prosperity? We've heard about it, we have even seen it, we aren't stupid, we look around, but how does prosperity work? If it is that common, shouldn't we have it too? At least be able to obtain it? After those monstrous killers back home, no, that isn't your fault, we aren't throwing that in your face, we are throwing ourselves in front of you, after they took everything from us we should be able to get something, anything back, no? Something should be accessible to us, we should get something, instead you call us a cursèd raging brood, brood, brood! Like animals! Brood of foreigners! That's what you call us and apply local means of atonement, where no sin was committed and the land has no more means. No one can be freed from ancient bloodguilt that horrifically escaped earth's womb, to us of all people, to my family, no exception made, besides me, I am beside myself, all dead, all dead, horrifically escaped guilt, but you don't care, you don't give a damn, all destroying—I can't read that: murdergene? No, we know nothing about genes, we were farmers, we were engineers, we were doctors, men and women, nurses, scientists, we've been something, yes, whatever it was, and now we must follow this brochure, which exists in several languages, while we must not exist even once, now we must read through this brochure and read it again and again. That is why we gratefully praise our memory, in whose service we are, since we can always only see the dead and get distracted like drivers by a cellphone call, and therefore we don't understand this brochure. As much as we try, please be patient, someone will tell us who the people are we are so different from and the ones who just showed up here unexpectedly; and what you see in us that makes us so alien to you; and why we and not our enemies have been marked for bloodguilt and so forth!, but you don't want to know any of that, and yet, over time one learns to even understand it, whatever it may be. The point is: one gets it at some point. Or not. Forgive me, please, we know, of course, that people are not fond of wordy speeches such as mine. Thank you very much. The brochure is brief and clear and not limited only to the specific circumstances, it is limitless, it applies to all, thus your superiority over us. What you say applies to all, to all, all and everyone, therefore also to me, you have poured all your intentions into one formula and now you can't get your intentions out of this formula. You pull and you pull on your intentions but no one can see a thing, the visibility is restricted, and that ghost driver approaches too fast in the fog. We feel really sorry for you! The specific circumstances, the deputies, the representatives of your circumstances are still too limiting for you, besides the awful limitations set by traffic regulations. Mustn't take the high road in the wrong direction. We can see that.

Besides, it is written right here, yes, here. We lie on the cold stone floor, but this comes hot off the press, here it is, irrefutably, irreconcilably, poured into this brochure like water that instantly runs down and out instantly, like water thrown from cliff to cliff, turned into water as well, sinking like statues, almost elegantly, with raised hands, no, no, from dam to dam, into the bottomless, into the micro power plant, down, down it goes for years, we vanish, we vanish as

we become more and more, funny, we still vanish, though
our numbers increase, our courage does not vanish, there
are ever more, though also fewer and fewer of us, many
don't even arrive, the suffering people are falling like water
off the cliff, down the butte, into the chute, over the mountains, through the sea, over the sea, into the sea, always
thrown, always driven, for years they swim, they drown, they
crash, they suffocate in cold storage wagons, die in aircraft
wheel wells, fall into highway toilets, fall from balconies, yes,
people like us!, they are all like us!, most of them plunge into
unconsciousness, right past your unconscience, honorable
hosts, dear motorists, often oppressed by speed limits, oh,
would those not exist! They are such a pain! Sorry, I must
have already said that somewhere. Equal in honor, it is the
basis of action, no, what are you saying? So this is what you
think of us! You say we don't care about honor, about dignity, we just want to come here, to come all the time never
to leave; you are saying: Once they are here, they are a drain
on our pocket, we'll prevent that and we are doing it right
now, oh dear, they are falling, they are untouchable, we don't
catch them, they drown, they drop, they dread, they quake,
earth quakes, regardless of lineage, gender, age and education, cut loose from everything, they are on their way to us,
no matter how they look or where they come from, future
pointless, past expired, here you have it black on white and
it is right!,—looks, discrimination and racism have no place
here with us, origin has no place here, at least none it would
give up, origin does not give up anything, it doesn't give, it
doesn't pay, racism has not found a place either, it must
stand, serves it right, serves everyone right, doesn't matter

that so many have to stand, that way more people can squeeze into the wagon, oh, and men and women are on equal footing, I am sorry, I forgot to mention that before, their votes count the same, one like the other, their voices sound, no, count the same, one like the other, it's written right here, when they cast their votes they count the same, children also have rights, but they don't count, they don't know how, not yet, but once they can count they don't count either, they are protected, they are protected by us, such attention, attention!, requires non-violent handling, they topple, they fall, yes, children too, they also become people after all, which we should prevent unless they are ours; in any case: Everything falls, there is nobody left to reset the trap after it has snapped shut, no one to stop the falling, to shoot the falling, though everyone has a smartphone at hand, ready to shoot, always ready, a must for any human interaction: gotta be ready to capture anyone, with our smartphones, which are smarter than us, which doesn't take much; everyone can capture everyone else, everyone stays, everything sticks and will be held onto, we hold them up high, our phones, like the government upholds the equal treatment of all citizens, everyone holds something, up high, what are you are holding up high here? Oh, I see, everybody holds the iCam, it guides your decision where to fly, drive or eat. Great. All are equal in front of the camera, even if not all have the same camera, but they all have one, children too, children also have rights and the iCam too and also the swipe screen, they'll be great thieves some day, whatever they see, swipe it and gone, and now they also take pictures with it!, attention, human dignity! Watch out, human dignity is also coming. Here it comes!, take a picture, quick, before it's gone again. Dignity, attention!, you should pay attention to it, or you'll miss it!, request that the State treat people who are in the same situation the same way!, okay, then why did that one, that foreigner get a seat in the subway and I didn't, how come he got in sooner than I?, he should always only get out!, how about values?, about falling?, how about any-thing?, how about it all? Well I'll push that one from the plat-form first chance I have I'll push him down, and it's like he's never been, if he isn't rescued. If he is rescued, he is free again, but not I, oh no!, was that rescue really necessary? I under-stand, freedom can be a feeling, I am telling you, a feeling, not everyone has it, sports know that feeling, nature does too, the skier in the mountains knows it, that is, everybody knows the feeling of freedom, everyone knows the feeling, everybody knows it, freedom!, that's all we need now!, yes, that is what we need, let us get out, unforced, undefeated, from the cleaned-up desk let's make a clean break, we need the freedom for free time, freedom is what we need, yes, that one there, sorry, nothing's left, I wanted to save some for you and suddenly it's all gone. I take this freedom and that freedom and suddenly nothing is left, I left no freedom for myself, bad deal, no, that other one's better, I'll take it, what?, someone else got it already? That's outrageous! Well, then I take the freedom next to it, even though someone has already reserved it, I take the liberty to use other people, no, to put them to good use, uh, wrong, it's freedom I put to good use, I use it so I can condemn, uh, condone the freedom of others, but not other people, I have no use for them, it's freedom I can use, yes!, to acknowledge, respect

and honor freedom, which can also be taken as freedom of
opinion and squeezed like a lemon, nothing left once everything's been pressed out; but not much was there to begin
with; I have taken the liberty of having my own opinion, but
now nothing's left, all gone, my opinion too, oh dear, pardon
me, did I take all the liberties? But here are some I just threw
out, you can have those! There must also be some in
the trashcan. I am not so bad, you can have them, they must
still be good. You can drown, suffocate, freeze, starve, be
beaten to death, all beautiful liberties, if not yours, but
maybe you are generous enough to pass them on? Thank
you. Thank you much. You know you are free not to share
my opinion. Great. I wouldn't share it anyway, at least not
with you! For no one decides over me, my opinion and my
life, except myself, and I certainly won't decide to let you
decide that I share my opinion with you, you won't even get
a small bite from it, I certainly can decide with whom I share!
You should have expected that, when the light twinkled
before it went out. I am going now too. They call for me
everywhere. No one called you, forever benighted as you
are, go back to your God with your stupid olive branch, get
out with your whole tribe, just die, dangle from a noose, in
New Zealand, wherever, or, if you prefer, get lost online,
plug yourself in. That's too loud, can't you turn it down?
You can't? Unheard of! You Gods up there, pull the plugs!
And what about that cruel hatred here? What does it want
here? It is wrong here. It's written right here, it's wrong.
Freedom ends where yours begins, yes indeed, but yours
doesn't begin, I'll take care of that, and mine doesn't end.
That's that. Yours ends before it begins and mine doesn't

end. And that's that. No. Not that! Come on now! Don't give me that.

But you can see it right here, really, right in this paragraph which includes us too, can't you see us?, don't you see us lying where we dropped?, we are lying down, but we are right in here too, we must read it: that we are not allowed to lie down, maybe some other place, but not here. Here lying is *verboten*, it ruins the lawn, it soils the water, if we had any, it pollutes the ocean, if it were here it would make sure it isn't!, it must be *verboten* wherever we lie, we have to lie somewhere, and that ultimately harms humans as such. You wrote it, it means something, now stand up for it! No, you don't have to stand, but you don't have to lie down either, okay, we lied down on the church floor, because God is there for everyone, lawmakers have defined that border, your God ends where ours begins, that's like freedom, no one can intervene not even the State, except when he has the urge to intervene in our areas of freedom, oh no, now he has the urge, he wants to cleanse us, so now the state opens his floodgates and passes his water all over us, still more water, thanks a lot, that's all we needed!, well, he had the urge, and just now it's really urgent, he has to let go, he just has to, he has to, he respects living together, but he decides with whom, he says who can live together and who can't, and then he respects that, but only within certain limits, beyond those he doesn't have to respect it, he is the only one who doesn't. For example, while swimming. This example has been chosen expressly, but what does it want to express? No, that's too stupid. What's with swimming? A neck-to-neck race? So that we can express our mutual respect afterwards?

Why must we first get into the water, slippery from spilled diesel, sinking, slithering through foreign fingers like fish in order to be recognized? We could just as easily drown right away, get bludgeoned already in the boat, get sick, or just die, have a still birth and the dead stuff gets thrown out, yes, that happens occasionally, be pushed off a platform, get hammered, no, wrong region, wrong religion, we could just as well get clobbered, all at once or individually, but why do we have to get into the water for that? Yes, some of us are getting out of the water, where accidentally, they did not starve to death, die of thirst or drown. But they don't want to get back into it. They don't want to go back. Once you have seen that much water, you don't want to get back in again just to fight by the same rules as the other one who made the rules, yes, I acknowledge your accomplishment, it wasn't bad, your accomplishments are always bigger than mine, I admit, it is important for our coexistence, in sports, in the family, in day-to-day life, that your accomplishments are always bigger than mine, I can see that. How come? Simply because you are bigger than I, your accomplishments are also bigger. This fair play of living so that one can die any time, the other one too, not any time but in his time, everything in its time, yes, living that way is the precondition of justice. We are all for harmonious togetherness, certainly, it is up to everyone's individual responsibility, we are like each and everyone, we are not yet dead, and therefore all set to stand on the same ground, if it's not too small, we are not a statue, we are not a state, not even of mind, no one here uses his mind, we just stand there, on our common ground, it is a foundation of values, called equivalency, yes, that's how values are put together. Why should I even stand up, if all have equal value? I lie here in the church, on the cold stone floor and I am worth as much as you! Believe it or not. You respect our diversity, we respect your exceptionality, though you are not particularly exceptional, except when it comes to making exceptions and exemptions, that is enlightened exceptionalism, which is exceptionally bright, though you are not, it is a blinding light, from one source only, that is the exceptional freedom of light, it has been calculated, the result was exceptionally unanimous, it has been frequently confirmed, it is being proven again right now and will soon be again, you'll see!, you'll see the light!, how bright it is, especially the unanimosity, sorry, unanimousness of our time!, which also applies to us, the time, not the light, for in-between it always gets dark again, this information is free, yes, time also applies to us, that's only fair and just, count me in when it comes to justice, I am in all the way, and even if it were possible to get a clear picture of someone else's death by being there, the way it got to that end would not be captured. You would not really get my end. You might bring it about, but you wouldn't get it. You can experience death on other folks, your own, sadly, only on yourself, and that's no longer an experience, well, I don't know, I could tell you things about death, about cutting off heads, about shooting, bludgeoning, knifing, it would ruin the fun of your own death, so then, end of referring to the death of others, now to yours: there is absolutely nothing you can do with your own death, no, nothing can be done about that, you can't get anything out of it, don't even try telling anyone about it, no one would believe you how it works, dying. You could never understand our endangerment, up there on your cliff, on your mountain, because the moment you are in such danger yourself, oops, it's too late. You don't understand it, but that would be the first step in creating a way for all of us being together, okay. But there can be no to be or not to be, just because you had to pee and didn't look to see if someone already stood there. We have no peers to stand up for us, but we are pissed on and told to piss off, though judged by the same rules, we are sentenced, we don't understand a line, we stand in line, we answer questions, we sign something, we write something, it makes no difference, all men are the same before the law, but law or not, it's all the same to you, same difference with the law that makes you the same, you just don't know: same as who. You only made it to Sesame Street. Real Estate. That was important to you. But then you ran out of money. Why everyone likes running so much is beyond us, we would love to stay.

Well now, does no one want to step on this foundation, up this cliff, from which we were meant to be thrown for years?, will no one climb in this boat, so we're not all alone here, we are all set to step on this foundation made of people, which is us, compacted, so many of us, you'd need an axe to split us apart again, piece by piece off our pile. Baked together, like bread, how can they pull us out again, through portholes, from the hulk that is us?, incredible, but not that one, we human lumps, no longer individuals, a human cake, a crude human block under your crude human wedge. All things imaginable exist in different ways, but we are fundamentally different existences who became one thing, which no longer insists on anything, as it must persist here, for nothing can tear us apart anymore, nothing can tear us away from each other anymore. For he who abides in foreign lands has lost his ties to his homeland. What does that mean? Who says that? The lack of those ties as such constitutes the unique intimacy of this relationship, which is homesickness. Home what? We didn't even know that home makes sick, no, that's all we knew, nothing else. In another homeland, a foreign land, no sickness, that's what we thought. That's how we imagined it. And the lack of ties to the homeland no one binds us to, what ties?, we are no neckties, we just stuck our poor necks out—so the lack of homeland can still exist on account of this relationship. Just about. That's it. Who says so? No one answers. The divers are coming to get us. Now they are looking after us, many thanks! We stand together, what else can we do, before they separate us. We only come in bulk, no longer individually, never again, even though they pull us out one by one. When will we be somebody again? We are all and nothing. We embrace each other forever. It is the foundation of living together and we do want to live together, with whoever it is, even with you if need be, if they let us, I mean, if it is permitted, that's what we want, it means everything to us, to be, to be something, to be a some-thing in front of this clear horizon, upon this foundation on which we build each other up, on which we build, on which we are not allowed to build but still do, so what, the permit will come later. You conveyed your values to us, thank you very much, we can read up on them, so now we step on this foundation of shared values, we want to get to know the fundament of this society, please tell us how we can get to this foundation, so that we can step on the fundament of values, that value base, before the values can step on us. They might want to climb higher. We must get to the first cliff, we must hang on to that. Otherwise it would be too high a step for us, from us, the unknown and ignorant folks, to you; we want to be a part of it, we want to be a part of this society, yes!, exactly!, we want to be cordially invited, and we most definitely will not think it's just for kicks, so we can be kicked off the fundament of your values again, like from a cliff, we, cliff-hangers on the evening news, that wasn't necessary, we've been kicked around and off elsewhere and that was something else, we know all about it, those fundamentalists, they want to throw us down, sure thing. A kick-off is what we need, if not this one, no, but with a ball, otherwise we stand still, we get stuck, we want to stand for your values, absolutely, in the workplace, in school, in vocational schools and in the family, which I no longer have, they are all dead, we have videos of two of them as they were beheaded, we'd love to stand up for your values wherever you like, for we know you wouldn't behead anyone, you wouldn't behead us or anyone else, except if someone's coming on to you the wrong way, but then it must have gone really wrong, because that's a lot of work, that's a tall order, but in the end it's a success, for no one can live without a head, that's a sustainable success and sustainability is important to you; we also want to get into your public swimming pools and if you don't kill us in time we'll be there, we'll dive in headlong and then we'll start swimming, and then we'll observe the rules of the swimming competition, and then other rules, then the right of way, we can do that too, we can do that, that's not dangerous, we want it all, we really want it, we want to fill work, school, leisure time with life though not with ours, we have too little of it and gave too much already, we couldn't even get an old-fashioned whirligig going with it, not a single one, and how many are left anyway. We, the dead, the relatives of the dead who lived with the dead, we want to fill your values with life, so at least they can live, we want to fill the base with life, which rests on diversity, by all means, by any means, that's what we want. They are all dead, but we want to fill the base with a life that has value, we want to fill values with life, so that they have a base, we want, we want, we are wanting. We want to be. We want to get rid of our inner problematic, and then we want to stand tall on your values, by all means, they already mean a lot to us too, yes, they mean our lot, no doubt. Especially to us, the dead, your values mean a lot, it's all we have. We have no choice. What base other than human dignity have we got? All dead. All dead. Equal in value, but dead, beheaded in front of a camera, those are small and light, easy to handle, smaller and lighter than the earth above or under us, everything becomes light and easy, the earth too, also the water above us, from where they pull us, we don't resist, we are light, everything is made light and easy for everyone in case it's not light enough, that's why we won't lie down underneath, because maybe whatever will come down on us won't be as light and easy as we thought. But our relatives, they faced it all, they were put in front of a camera, it clicked, it was turned on and aimed at them and then their heads were cut off. The boat was full and then we made a quick exit on it. Which regulation tells us how to find our way in this opaqueness, this mass of water? You see, no, luckily you don't see and still it is true: Human dignity, important at the beginning and the end of life is not a property, a quality, no, not a property, it is the result of our existence as humans, and if we are not human, we have no dignity, if we have no dignity, we are not human, oh no, no one human is one of us, how lucky for him!, but that's exactly what we were dying to be! Every one of us, to be! That is not the question anymore. The clearest eyes shine also in the dark and you can see: not possible. We want to be here, yes, we have different talents, which we offer like gifts, like the heads of the dead, of our dead, we offer our talents, they are our mode of payment, we don't have any other. And that method is outdated, it has expired long ago, like our breath.

Our existence is our currency, it's all we have, in other words, we have nothing, we have our existence as payment, but we are no cash cow, not by any means, that is Mrs. Yumasheva, her name is written right here, spelled correctly I hope, daughter of Yeltsin, yes, a daughter, instantly naturalized, she had it made, she made all the payments, and if not herself, then someone else did it for her, the recognition and acceptance of the uniqueness of a human being has been paid for, it must always be paid for, this daughter has been paid for, maybe not by herself, someone must have paid to make justice possible on the large and not only on the small scale, so she may live here, this daughter of Yeltsin—he has faded in the meantime, back then he might have still been rosy, no rather reddish in full bloom, but I don't think so, I'd have to check, I don't have the time, to get that checked someone probably will have to pay for that too—fixing up an Opel plant with a Russian bank must be paid for, fixing and making cars must be paid for and when someone buys the car, it's time to pay again. I respect any form of payment that's been made so that this daughter can live here, I respect it by forming my own action accordingly: I don't pay, I could not pay anyway, therefore I have no right to be here, I do not pay and I cannot do so, I can't pay and I won't pay. Or the other one, the Russian soprano, Anna, not Tony, we dedicate her to all foreigners, we are happy to share, though she is not. Laurel crowned, she shares neither fruit nor fright: a well-rounded body of sound, as that of the other daughter takes a lot of voices but only one invoice, and that in turn was covered by her voice, we all want to sound harmonious, don't we, and for that voice we need a lot of voices, which we don't have anyway, but also the voice of this second daughter, yes, her, who comes from far away; her home-land's mountain forest no longer stares at her, she is with us now, she has arrived, or not? Not yet? All fees have been paid for her and she came, not enwrapped in fugacious fumes, not spit out of gathering clouds, not sprayed by dew-covered mountain forests, let alone with lots of noise, no, she would not have wanted that, loud and tiring noise. Better quiet. Her residence is here now and her suite, her chambers are here, just another old shack in the borderland, not even the owner ever saw her, not once; then, probably later, some-thing blurs my vision, couldn't be fear, a burglar-proof—whatever—flat, villa, mansion, all paid, that's later, when she's actually there; first she dwelled there, alone or not alone, with spouse, with child, without, with without, what-ever, she isn't even here, but that's where she'll be riding in

after having ridden out the battle fought in the fatherland's
customary fashion and the fatherland's citizens' decision,
that's where she'll be surfing in on her fatherland's con-
verging streams of money, doubtful whether she'd find
comfort with her father, he might already be dead, congrat-
ulations, that certainly wouldn't get to her, instead she'll get
here on account of the man who paid, but she isn't here yet,
please be patient for a moment, first there, soon here, with
us, where she wanted to be, where she just felt like being,
always standing on legal grounds no one ever had against
her, there she is, where wild desire carried her, no idea why,
she is there, that's all, but now she suddenly is here, in a flash,
we are amazed, no, no hot flash, she still is in the heat of her
youth, in the company of husband and child and in the
meantime she might not even be here anymore, whatever.
She has been paid for and now she's here or maybe gone
already, the lost one, the found one, I speak of shadows, I
speak to the water, it spits at me in response and also spits
me out again some time, I know, I know, she is one of those
in our homeland's holy groves, who must not become one
of ours, no, we don't mean this woman, we don't know anymore whom we mean, yes, now we know again, we mean a
secure homeland which we don't get, which that woman
already has and already left again, just left it, maybe without
having ever been there. A God, deep in secret darkness, no,
not in a dungeon, he is not endangered like us, has paid for
her, but there's only one God, our God won't pay, not for us
at any rate, not for a homeland, happy the daughter, the
lucky one!, who still has hers, perhaps she already moved
away, the new homeland stamped into her passport, paid and

stamped, the lucky one, it was bought for her, the new homeland, that's also hard work!, however, it is the work of others, no matter, the main thing is it will get paid and has been paid. Do not flee from me! Why should I, says the daughter: *Wehe dem Fliehenden, Welt hinaus Ziehenden! Fremde durchmessenden, Heimat vergessenden, Mutterhaus hassenden*, uh, woe to the runaway, traversing worlds away, forsaking his native land, hating his motherhouse—motherhouse?—, a monastery?, *Mutterhaus* for parent company ?, nonsense, it's all in a song, sorry, Franz, all lost in translation, I am not one of those runaways, if I hadn't had that *Mutterhaus*, I certainly wouldn't be here now, and I am also sure that my security has been insured and paid for; mother's house, father's house? Blossoming with no ground to stand on? Properties not proper for us? Not there to prop us up? Memories, gathered in a school, a gym, a community center, a church? Uniqueness, uncomfortable for everyone? We, comforted by no one, except with blankets, sleeping bags and jogging suits. Yeltsin. A ruler. And that's good. That one: don't know her, not the other one either, no, don't know her, never heard of her, what's this all about? *Freunde verlassende folget kein Segen, ach, auf ihren Wegen nach.* Forsaking friends no blessing will follow, oh! on the ways they later will go!—On the contrary! Don't know anything about it, didn't happen to me, no god hinders my flight, I am not a cow, I am not Europa, not Io, nothing hinders me, one or another fucks me or not, he has a choice, it's been paid, and here I am now, exactly where I wanted to be. If I am not completely mistaken, I am getting insulted! No, I am not the one who is speaking here, and no one is insulting me either.

Behold the one who was has been paid for, here she is, the new one, from heaven high she came to earth, on eagles' wings, no, sorry, by plane, she arrived on an airplane, out of her homeland's darkest night into her new homeland's bright light of day, this land that's your land, that cannot be mine, but is already hers. No word that drives the fog away from us, we can see her bright and clear, this woman who came to earth by plane, no word from us can drive the fog away, every one of her words drives everyone else away, only the money stays, the money she pays off with, stays. Even as a cow she would still be beautiful, even transformed, traversing our meadows, even as a cow!, what pasture, pray tell, what cattle track do you belong to, woman? She likes to tell: created from earth, but here now, legally here, supported by sponsors, how suspicious! But no one cares, shame—unknown to anyone here—always yields to love, because it was paid for, lump sum, no lumps taken, and now she is here, she'd rather not be seen as a cow, which she is not, though her flanks are the softest. That this woman is allowed to harmonize with us, well, not with us, we could get in harm's way, we must not whisper, we must not wail, we can't do anything, not even be here, but that woman can, maybe we could sing too, with her body of sound, in her body of sound, maybe we can do it that way, let's try, body masses sliding into each other like mountains, the earth quakes, buildings collapse, relatives die, are dug out of the ground barehanded, then back into the ground, but this woman's sounds resound, the hills are alive with her sound, this seduced beauty, who instantly had the land at her feet, what a sound! She sounds as if lit by hundred eyes, I mean

the other one, both daughters of another land, both bright
and therefore here, both can trust us, ever vigilantly, the land
spies on us, but it leaves out those two, those daughters don't
have to show any papers, because they have something to
show, those two, yes, money the one, voice the other, her
wonderful voice, here she is, she simply belongs here, can't
do without her, imagine this voice resounding some other
place, which it does, but she belongs to us, the daughter and
her soapy soprano, beg your pardon, that was even lower
than usual, I don't care, I don't have to listen to it, okay, so
she got the residence permit, she can rest wherever she
wants, she gets in anywhere, the other one too, of course.
They may graze during the day, but once the sun drops from
the sky, the guards do not lock them up either, not like us,
the two daughters can do what they want, no humiliating
rope holds them back by the neck, so they can't drink from
the muddy brook, or drown in the ocean like us, the dear
one, the precious one, neither daughter shall suffer, let them
stay here and keep quiet or sing, that's up to them, it's all
paid for already, paid for one, the other climbs the hills
resounding with music and sings, fantastic, no one ever saw
such horns, heard such music!, here, go ahead, feel it, if you
don't want to hear it, but you definitely want to hear her,
we swear! You want to hear her, everybody approaches her
admiringly, we, however, we, however, a talking train into
nothingness, we, however, our foot marks in the sand, but
no traces remain, we are marked, marked by dust, sticky
from sea water and gasoline, stuck together by the narrow-
ness, welded together by too much closeness, but we, a pain
in the snow-white neck of the groaning cow, seeing the

breakneck champs in the deep snow, untouched, everything
untouched, everything whiter than white, but we, we touch
no one, and no one would touch us, okay, we must remain
silent and that stands to reason, for everyone denies us an
answer. Our words, only sighs, squeezed from the depth of
the heart, are denied an answer, we give everything to the
spokesman, we give him every information, but no one
wants any, everyone wants to hear only the one daughter
singing and not hear the other at all, that one has been paid
for, oh, unknowing us!, okay. That daughter now sings here
in a choir, be happy! We'll be happy for you if you don't
want to be happy. You want to hear it? Wonderful! Enjoy!
But we? The locked doors of death expand our sorrow from
eternity to eternity. Hear the song, brief and clear, listen to
it, it is our song and thus you probably can't hear it, that
might be the reason: we may not pride ourselves as foreigners, while the granddaughter of that ecstatic cow, oh well,
some kinship must be there, I'm sure, I just forgot which,
daughter?, dragged to remote, if hearty pastures? And no
guard sitting there, not one who watches from the moun-
taintop what she is doing, what she is up to, what she wears;
we, on the other hand, they follow us, they watch us,
because we slipped through the ocean's nets, because we
shipped ourselves to the wrong address where we never
arrived, where we would have put our stamp on a house, a
room of our own, where we would have moved in and
moved things around, we are under surveillance, because
we messed up the lawn in front of the church with our junk,
destroyed its pretty green coif, forever. For once, please, just
once pay attention to me, who saw to it that, truth be told,

that the truth of this report is being made up as we speak,
all lies, for a small fee, that's more than enough for that fee-
fi-fo humbug, believe it or not. Of course you believe it.
Men-weaned, human-blood-craving amazons is not what
we'd take you for, says a politician who knows, who's been
to famous Babel more than once, who knows a thing or
two, the politician, he talks, many are talking, that one's also
talking, I don't know his name, we wouldn't take you for
women, he says, first off, because you are men, you are men
as well, whatever you are, yes, women too, children too, let
the little ones come to me, we swiftly revoke their being if
they call for their mommy, we drown them and on top of
each coffin we put a little teddy bear. Yes, we top it off with
more! Five coffins, five teddies! That'll do. They probably
never had those before. They had no coffins to play with and
no teddy bears. We withdraw them and they withdraw from
us, we swiftly avoid what was sent to us. Delivery refused.
If you were archers, you would be just archers, if this
woman weren't Yeltsin's daughter, she'd just be a daughter
that's all, just anybody, not one struck by lightening, or
drowned in the sea, basically she would be like one of our
relatives, just different, not beheaded like my cousins, that's
what I mean, a naturalized immigrant, that's how it works,
that's how it goes, a citizen, not a supplicant, she doesn't
need protection, she doesn't need surveillance, no need for
a shepherd herding her running wild through hallways, she
is already a citizen, became a citizen just recently, but forever,
masterminded by the CEO who abducted her on her way
here, blowing through taut blades of grass, no whistle
blower he, he just blows through blades, and also through

tubes; he fetched the daughter, not his, a daughter, not any daughter and not his, just: the daughter, because he wanted the car company, not at any price, but at one he can pay. His own company, the subcontractor, which is far from contracting, on the contrary, it's not enough for him anymore, everybody wants more, many want it all, he does too, he wants it all, we can see that, he brought her here and paid for her, for nowhere is the grass greener and the shepherd enjoys any shadow that falls on him, no, he does not enjoy this one, he doesn't care, the company guy, who's in the can now, candied, for his life is sweet, no, sorry, he is a candidate, the candidate cherry on a humongous cake, which is him, which he built himself, a man in the middle of wedding cake buildings, isn't his apartment in *Zug*, what?, on a train?, a *Zug* to Zug?, Switzerland?,—who can stand it so long in either *Zug*?, whatever!, —*Zug* also stands for draught, so that's where it is, an apartment on the *Zug*, in *Zug*, in the *Zug*, in the draught, wherever!, the answer is blowing in the *Zug*, you said it!, it sucks, that makes slumber shy away even from us, there is his place, but that's not a home, he's never there, his softly cradled slumber never guarded, never shadowed, that man is everywhere and nowhere, but he definitely isn't there, not anymore, probably never, above that supermarket in Zug, he had never been seen there, like the daughter who is to bring the company here has never been sighted in her squalid little house, she has a better one, I've been told by a god, whose hundred eyes—out of numbness and boredom, because the same thing keeps happening over and over again—are already drooping in part, always the same, always the same, but elsewhere it's always elsewhere, where

another part keeps watch, but none in Zug, Zug has no part
of this man, but Zug has it coming, its share, it will get its
own little share, and that one he won't share, because he'd
have to pay more with us here, it's very little there, ask him,
go ahead, ask him, whoever finds him, ask him how he was
discovered, he was found, we, however, nobody cares where
we are, they couldn't care less about anything, there, where
it says Zug, there, on the *Zug*, no, not our pitiful, freezing
Zug—our train, our column, also called *Zug* in that land—,
there in that beautiful train there are many, but again, no
one's in the apartment, at least not that man, he must leave
the land, he may return, but only for a short time, we aren't
worried, we know he'll be back; so he'll come, here he is,
on TV, teeing on the golf course, on the race track, racing,
no, but he's there too, and then gone again, at the right time,
that takes some figuring, and all for him, that figures!, the
finance guys want it that way, they even require it, why not,
in, out, in, out, why not, it's great to have some variety, fairness is more important, but variety also counts, a band, yes,
our entire state orchestra has been enriched by this cool
player and it's the same in many other areas of daily life. The
man is loaded and now he gets us loaded, onto a draughty
old train we don't belong here, we are not entitled to your
mountains, your lakes, there is no sea and the people here
don't want to see us either. He could do something else too,
that man who brought the cow down from cold mountains,
where else would gods want to dwell but in the shady woods
when it gets hot, and in shady orchards, when they get
hungry? Where? Where to dwell? That one? Dwelling? Well,
here and there, you can look in Zug, on the *Zug*, you can

look in Canada, in Russia, you can look everywhere and he will be everywhere, he does everything for us, well, not for us but for all the others here, those he wants to enrich with himself so he can enrich himself, but not those, no, not those, who fled to us through impassable deserts, calm streams, sandy lands and impossibly deep oceans. We, however, we. We, yes, we.

The man who talks such high-blown talk and has all talk reported to him like a fire, is really valuable as a fellow human being, he is incredibly valuable, which no one can imagine but he, that man and what he does is as valuable as a Hershey's bar, as valuable as a glass of milk, a very small one, invaluable, depends what for and to whom, valuable to us all, to the community, any contribution is valuable and if the man is not elsewhere but here, he is valuable to us and when he is elsewhere, he is valuable to others, maybe to himself, who knows, why not, why not? We don't know any corporate bosses, we don't know anyone, not even ourselves, does anyone know himself?, who knows the ropes? It won't do, nothing will do, even though we make do with so little, no one naturalizes us, we have no one behind us, no one with a corporation, we don't even have someone behind us with a single-family house, well yes, sure, maybe we do have that one, he also wants his role in this environment, wait a minute, he's still looking for it, he'll find it any moment, maybe he finds it with us, who knows? This corporate king found his part in ostracizing, no, sorry Austrocizing this daughter of a cow, no, of a bull, no, there's no bull, no red one in all this bull either, anyway, a star was born. Or did this cow come about some other way? A metamorphosis? Who knows. All that's left is to report the talk, to report this nymph, for us to report at homeland, not ours, at homeland security, the buck stops there, that's where we end, like the cow cut off from water on her flight. But why would she do that? She is already here. Why flee? Once a womb's young sprout, now a womb herself. That's her! Hello! Though once you fugitives seemed to have had a share of this land, oh no, those were others, now we are being questioned and we can't blame others now, it would just be excuses, they ask, snatching up answers like gasping for air, for the answer means nothing to them, it is like the wind sighing above them, like the water they are under, which is crashing above them, until they are revealed again, pulled out, wrung out, laid out, no thoughts of them passed on, although those thoughts were there. Now they are things, same as other things, adjusted to the void, the water, an unequal fight with this element, to swim or not to swim, that is the question, and so they ask: But what caused you to flee the house of the fathers? Yes, that's what we ask ourselves. Not only you ask us this, we ask too, only whom? All dead. They are all dead now, and when there was time to ask, we didn't have any questions. We still don't. Time we do have, but nothing, no one else. Now. For example, we have, it is just an example, that is all we have, we don't even have a phony residence in the safe haven of Zug, a tax haven, above the supermarket, lots of people there, no one in the apartment, they should spread out better! But we spread out here, where alms are handed out, that's not how we imagined it, but that's what happened. While a god listens ecstatically to the newly invented musical art of this singer who became a citizen, she already was a singer before, she was lucky, wasn't she?!, our soft whisper does not reach his ear, of course not, our lisped lament does not reach his desk, how could it, how? We are not sitting at the hearth of our palace, which was a hut, which was a little house, not that little, which was something, whatever, which does not count here, we are no longer sitting there, where we were, so the whole city bears the guilt of our lot.

The water bears the guilt, the water carries the debt, bless you both, that you pay me more than the interest, that you pay with your capital, with people who came here as the method of payment for themselves, I'll take them, do you have more of them? Or have you already enough of them? This question surges up in me, and so I am on my way, the path that follows me, the dear water, or is it the other way around? Do I follow a path? Could be, since so many are riding my waves and rise like suns and then go out. I vaporize them. Good riddance. They rise above me and away. The city bears the guilt, God bless, dear guilt, I am the city, I am happy you exist and happy to be your carrier. Nothing to speculate here, not electricity, not telephone wires, not fiber optic cables. Nothing to carry from or to, nothing to carry on about, no one gets carried away and no one cares anyway. Well, I could also say something altogether different. Nothing to be conducted except that woman and she has long been naturalized, yes, we've already said it and, yes, that other one too, because the art of music should be brought—and kept—in close contact with the people, yes, I've said that before, but no one's interested. After the fight according to the fatherland's custom, which means, none at all, she is already naturalized, the other one too, done deal, we are not, that's dead certain. She has been made a citizen, naturalized against payment, the other for a song, the first one a citizen as per payment and amortization of a certain lump sum, the other for payment by voice and real estate. She has been naturalized and paid, that woman, the daughter, that maiden's name I don't recall, I am afraid I never knew it, no, I did, I wrote it down but now I can't find it—Neb—Neb—no, not nebbish, that lovely name, doesn't matter, she is here now and may stay as long as she wants to, even though she is no longer here, she may stay, with passport and stamp, not collapsed in front of our eyes, she can stand her ground, for never did she hold legal grounds against this land. She really didn't. Not like us, we have grounds, but those are not legal grounds. Where the law starts the ground ends, any ground, any property, that's the so-called legal-property boundary and it runs: exactly here. Exactly! According to the law, pass judgment on me, on the gods' protection here and on those who can bypass the law. We can't. Pass judgment on us. We can do nothing. The daughter, however, Yeltsin's daughter, that much we do know, her name, you can see it right here, we forgot it, sorry, but she was here for a short time only, until she had her passport and the fun that comes with it, but you also can look up her name elsewhere, if you like, I've had enough of looking things up, in my case others are looking for lots of things, yes, the one who had the right to legal residence, even the law itself paid for her, paid by the corporate king, yes, he, who now runs for some higher office, we don't yet know exactly what, but he must know, you, corporate king, you?, this land's chancellor?, why not, from our perspective, we don't have a say anyway, but your name—Yeltsin—no, not that one for once, you, man of Now and man to come, it's your name I know, you produce sound and smoke, and at a high price at that, mind you: the production is difficult and complicated, the sales price therefore all the higher, but still, no Opelia, and no soprano for you. Forgive me, I get carried away some times, but the cow stays, for the time being she'll stay, don't you want to take care of us? Yes, care, you! Take care of an insurance policy. You and your vassals, make sure we are feeling good, as good as the daughter in the empty house in the Burgenland border villages of Upper Wart or Lower Wart, she waits out the qualifying period in a place far away from the refugee quarters in Upper Wait or Lower Wait, she isn't stupid, she waits in Between Waits, in the waiting area, but in a nicer place, and if the Swiss apartment is too small, too empty, too much above the supermarket, then we just won't stay there, that's obvious. Why should we?

You, Sir, in Switzerland, in Canada, in Austria, lord of spare parts, lord of all stocks, I mean of the entire stock, unfortunately you didn't get it all, it surely isn't our fault you couldn't transform the maiden into a cow, uh, I mean the body parts into one big cash cow: one whole car, all those operations for the Opel for nothing, futile I think, as futility is the lot of us all, sadly, because participatory democracy does not just mean casting one's vote in elections, better not having a vote, then one wouldn't have to go there, because democracy is so much more than that, you recognized that with your party, we recognized nothing, but it doesn't matter,

we can't vote anyway, we can't even vote where we put up
our bed, you lord of the failed car purchase, I mean the purchase of the car factory, you didn't get it, you didn't get the
Opel plant, despite all the offerings, none of those a gift,
except one, a gift for the Yeltsin daughter, a great gift, and
still you are our overlord, even though you give us nothing,
nada, not like Jesus, but still lording it over us to a tune we
can't sing but that woman can. Quickly listen to the nodding
woman, who nods everything through, even the tyrant, also
when it's a go, because the point where the head is attached
to the neck, that is where her tones originate, her wonderful
singing, and we, the bleeding ones, are blown away, thrown
off the cliff, out of awe when we hear her sing, off the cliff
with us that reddens all the while until we get down into the
water. You, lord of the empty flat in Zug, of the wedding-
cake castle some other place, where all that sweetness lives:
grace us with your omnipresent justice as you did for that
woman you transformed into a fellow-country-woman in
this countryside by a *blitz* ruling you took care of, the *blitz*
was your doing, Lord Almighty!, you took care of the ruling
in the special interest of the land, which exactly suits your
interests. This land is you, no, that's a bit too much, the land
allows you to introduce your ideas any time, but only you,
well, not quite the only one, but you as well, and especially
you, the land allows us nothing, we are nothing and it allows
us nothing, even though we would like to participate, it's
better than watching, no?, so that the law also comes from
us, so that the law also goes for the people, which we will
be then too, but the law does not come and go, and when it
goes out, it dresses up, it gets all decked out, but we may not

come along, we can't even get into the restaurant, that's not justice, even though justice would also come to us, at least it would if it could get some time off for once, and our dream act, unfortunately, passed far away, no, it's been shot here, the dream pass, by a soccer hero, local off-shoot of foreign parentage, he passed with flying colors, but now its no longer here, I mean the dream pass, it's been shot, and the hero does his dream act in Munich now with his passport of our dreams, but justice, which could also come to us, if we belonged to this dream-*Volk*, the people who shoot dream passes and have the passports we want so much, but don't get, but you, you, lord, you, man, king, you could not pin down the Opel either, no Sir, you wanted to, with the Russian Bank, that was supposed to work, deep in slumber's shadow you are still making money, even when you do nothing you are making money, but of course that's not true, you must work your butt off, we would too, but they won't let us. You moved the daughter of Zeus, no, the Czar's, you moved her in here and then you had her naturalized, you wanted to buy, well, at least we can buy pita bread, though we don't have to, we get it for nothing, we get food for free, good to be free, even if it's rotten, it rotted and, quite naturally, citizens are outraged about us getting spoiled bread, we shouldn't get anything, of course, but you for once were not spoiled rotten, your plan was spoiled, because you don't make five-year plans, no, that's not why, you couldn't be spoiled, though rotten, because Mommy Dearest, the dear corporate mother, General Motors, the general of motors, the top gun of the entire military, of the entire world with all the motors, all of them, well, almost all of them, she didn't allow it, oh lord, here you can see for once how it is and how it can happen even though the daughter is a citizen now, you paid but you got nothing for it, oh no, you'd never do such a thing, you don't invest in uncertain things, in objectionable objects, you invest with perfect wrath only when it's worth it, the daughter might have paid something too, we don't know, we wouldn't know, amidst the sparks of her precious stones she must have paid, they all pay, they can, everyone pays for what they can get, we, however, do not pay, nor are we methods of payment, but you, lord, master of all methods of payment, please pay for us too, be the State, lead it, pay for us, but no, you don't do that, you could pull off a blitz-naturalization, but you could not obtain the Opel, you see, oh lord, we pay, no, pray that you won't get the Opel, that's total nonsense, we know that of course, we've said it at least three times before, but it still isn't just. It drives the sting of madness deep into our chest, oh no!, that will drive us wildly around the globe. Nothing is just, you, State, are you at least just?, here, with us, you would have an object, you could practice justice on us, please, any time, we are ready, maybe you can finally master it and will no longer have to practice, but you are not, and you don't want to practice either. Be all just, as you are almighty, State, okay, just just will also do, all just even better, then he would be just to us all, pious and loyal, dear State, where we all want to be, our refuge, which you should become! Please help us!

Do not betray us refugees, please, please don't!, like, yes, exactly, like you did not betray that fugitive woman, daughter, with money, you did not betray how much, the way she stood there, knees bent, neck tilted backwards, but bought her, for how much!, you don't tell!, for how much you wanted to buy yourself with the bank into the car business, the plant, the greatest, the biggest ever, I think, okay, almost, but very big at any rate, from far away the nice giant GM looks at you benevolently, but he doesn't want to come here himself, unlike us, who were happy to come, and then he drops you, he, the biggest, much bigger than you, there always is someone bigger, you see, that's what also happens to us, except no one looks at us benevolently, no one looks at all, they don't want to see us, or the crap they feed us, the donated worn-out sofas, no, it's not yet straw-filled sacks we rest on, they don't see any of it, nothing at all—the way we prepare ourselves for participation in the democracy, if we could see it just once, just get a look at it!, withered our shoulders and hands, our hands dried out from doing nothing, a democracy, its hooves racing over us, nevertheless, it would be nice, at least we could see what's ahead of us and what we should prepare for, oh lord, lord of spare parts, for you never got the whole thing even though you paid a pretty penny, in addition to the all new citizenova, the cow, nothing left of the cow now, just the pure white shape, wherever she is, no idea, oh lord, so then do not betray us fugitives, as you did not betray that fugitive, the nymph, now happily naturalized, it's only natural that we like beautiful women, that nymph too, with her fast-climbing legs, our nationalized treasure, she hesitates to talk, we do not see her, who knows where she is, this land's new national, but we don't know where she stands out these days and how she looks, her bovine roar does not reach us here, we, however —our words cut off by fear—do not betray us fleeing ones, who are on earth but fleetingly, there isn't much to fork out for us, we won't stay too long either, we promise, even though we would like to, naturally, we, the expelled, please fork some over for us too, as you once forked over for the cow, your talk lots of dung, your wealth loads of it, please fork it out, not just for forklifts, please pay the price for us also, that's nothing for you, compared to the car plant, not to mention its mommy, the corporation in the USA, that would be too expensive even for you, can't buy that one, but us you can, as you could buy citizen- and sponsorship for the cow, in the shortest time, trying again and again, good man that you are, no, it works right away, with the right amount of money, everything works right away, that's the way to bring the goddess to the people. But as for the daughter company, the sons' company, whatever, lord, are we cheap compared to that, and you might even get a massive dis-count, we can handle massive workloads, as soon as more are coming, hundreds of thousands are coming, they are already here, they arrived, even if not right here, but they might come here, maybe all of them will come, that's the goal, at least theirs, come on in all of you, please, let the little children come to me! Hundreds of thousands, please come!, into the ocean if need be, there is still room, plenty of it, room for many more, let the little ones come to me, says the ocean, which is already big, come and go with the tide, though it could be a bumpy ride. Here they come to be taken for that ride and there they are coming together, now they stop, everything does, as a pasted-together, glued-together thing, one huge human chunk, in the water, we already bought the crude wedges; they are still coming as we speak, they are coming in droves, we can see them bright and clear, not dark and dirty, they are coming to mass, no, en masse, fear still tames them, but we can't guarantee they will come in the future, because here everything rests upon—it's written right here, let's say it right now, everything rests upon cooperation, participation, discussion, decision making, action taking, policy shaping and sharing accountability. And for all that there are quite a few more than a few and what's more is a lot more than less, that's obvious: the more the merrier. Yeah, well, in America they decided you don't get the plant, even though you wanted it so much, indeed, you've already done one good deed for it, planting good seed, so then, even though you wanted it, the plant, wanted it so bad, really bad, you raised your face to heaven and prayed and paid and put in a good word and had good words thrown into the pressure cooker, where they are boiling with rage now, oh lord, give us rubber to burn, give us Opel, I am the right boss for it, said you, we understand you well, and with your fundamental understanding of the Opel operation, you got it, you don't have to learn anything else for it, you got the understanding for the Opel world, we only for the *Opfer–*, the victim world, you, boss, for the Opel-world, for which you laid the foundation, on which to build the foundation for a new Opel plant: there is, however, more to turning a profit, profit alone won't do, there are too many plants, especially those, they will be shut down now, we, however, don't want to be shut down, we don't want to be shut up and in and deported, we want to grapple with background reports and backroom deals, before they grab us and separate us, because we gabbed too much during class. We want to get to the bottom of it, not the ocean, we just got out of there, but the whole deal, backroom deals, up-front cash, global connections, before they disconnect us, because we have not paid for the call. We don't stop talking, even though we should, this is a church!, we should be allowed to at least point out problems and solutions, no, we aren't, because we are not one of them and never will be, we can see that, even though we've already formed an opinion, but who wants to hear it and what does it look like anyway? We are not given to biases and prejudice, do you think we want to take over and that's the reason we are taken to hearings, frequently, constantly, mostly unexpectedly, taken like animals, driven like crazy through the hallways of the home that isn't ours. But here it says we should express ourselves openly and unprejudiced—oh, unprejudiced—not unperjured, that we are somebody, we are somebody who have an opinion and express it most expressively, we should not be afraid to express ourselves, the sighs, the tears, the nagging melancholy, we should leave it all behind, now we should express ourselves freely and openly, because an open mind will lead to a better understanding and that means making democracy possible, but it doesn't mean making the Opel purchase possible for you, Sir, not even with the Russian bank, not even with the savings bank that saves our money we don't have, but not theirs, not the bank's money, no expense spared there and not even if we get a Russian bank which was naturalized thanks to you and not even if we can bank on a new Russian neighbor on account of your express transfers, yes, the fantastic soprano, the beauty, that one too, of course, she really sings beautifully, like velvet, she really earned it, who if not her, also for the future, she deserves it forever and gets it too, oh, could we lie there for just a moment—no, not on top of her, not under her, what are you thinking—soft like that for an hour, where we could bed down, until we might possibly get a real bed some time. We are waiting, we are lining up, we keep in line, we stay on the line, our life is always on the line, countless Opel parts also get moved on an assembly line, excuse me, that also fits in here, doesn't it?, we wait unquestioningly for our questioning, we are looking for the wrong answers, we are told, we are constantly told, we are telling ourselves just now, because it was told to us. No question, they say, if we hadn't listened to the wrong side our trials would be over now, but we don't believe it, we have kept silent so often, and what happened?, nothing happened, we must all be on the same page, they say, so we can't turn the page either, then how can we check if we got the right answer? Which one is the right side, you think, oh Lord, excuse me, Lord Almighty, are you perhaps the wrong side to listen to? No, you cannot be, the lord is everything, he is every side, he is on every page, he is above everything, he can be turned anytime and there he will show us his real face and interests and critical insight, and he will acquisition something—it says so right here, so you can read up on it too—after he has already acquisitioned everything else, the good lord, he can also acquire art and culture, who cares. Not he. He'd be the last. He is not interested in art and culture, even though he says so. No way. Round eyes just get narrower, legs no longer aim to kick, screams no longer resound, if art were to resound, it would really be a problem, you'd hear nothing and no one anymore. If fear

cut off the word, we'd just try again. You, Sir, are you open
for the new, the foreign? No, you are not. But we are supposed to be, you, Sir, hear this: You are not president, but
verily, we say unto you, ask what you can do for others, not
what others can do for you! It says so right here. Isn't that
old stuff? Maybe, but it says it right here. We do not have
the words. We do not need them anyway, because that much
has been answered, it has been answered all by itself, it has
been answered without a hearing, and truthfully of course:
you naturalized the Russian princess, and others were also
supposed to do something for it, no idea what, but those others are in America, and they have done absolutely nothing
for you. You wrapped your arms around the Russian presi-
princess whom we had never heard of and brought her, got
her here, she still hesitates to speak, she says nothing, doesn't
live here, where she should live, she only rented, someone
else rented it for her, she did not have to come for it in person, she isn't even here, has never been here and now she's
gone again anyway. No one saw her. If anyone did, he should
report it immediately.

We, however, we could do something, we would love
to do something, though it might be the wrong thing, but
we would do something, for we could not stop the flight of
this maiden, who by now is surely somewhere else. Okay.
Everything always starts with rain. No, not the one in Spain,
that one makes people sing along, we are not allowed to
sing, we are not allowed to do anything, not even for a song,
we, of all people!, who would love to do things, good things
for you too; and that rain at that time, the rain of the century
was proof that we could not do anything, such rain is not

always a good thing, no matter whether we are doing something or not, so then we cast a wider net, but we did not get
a hold of anyone: Homeland Security, fire department,
national guard, neighbors helping neighbors, yes, you can
read it right here, they are all on their way, everything is running at full speed, there is an outpour in the downpour to
stop the flood—yes, also of people like us, we would, we'd
downright flood you if they'd let us, but we would also clean
up the flood, honestly, with our hair if necessary, and rubber
boots we'd surely get somewhere, and if the water came
down through the ether, we would turn off the gas taps and
stop the cash flow, you are quite right, everything, everything
has been mobilized to prevent floods, to prevent worse,
to prevent us, to prevent people, throngs of people from
flooding you, a veritable sea, a sea of troubles, sea to sea, sea
into sea, where they end, where they finally end up and
already there are fewer of them around, so then more and
more are coming, whole trainloads, in overloaded sinking
boats, they are coming and that must be prevented, we can
see that, folks like us must be barred, put in bars, no, behind
them, we don't drink, so that we won't flood you, no, no,
that must not be, that goes to show the importance of assis-
tance, of solidary collaboration against us, especially in times
of crises, that is when the floods of us must be prevented,
when you must be in solidarity with yourself, that's a must,
with whom else, first of all with yourself, yes and this is
when you help your neighbors, so we won't overrun you like
water, that's solidarity for you, readiness is all, for action,
naturally, because that is anything but natural, not a gift of
nature, yes and there it is, the readiness, bravo!, because you

apparently are always on duty, when it comes to breaking, jailing and finally shutting us in and remove us by plane, which always rattles, because they keep shooting, no, shutting us up, gagging one, then another and so those choked to death, and others too, for sure. That's what happens when you can't breathe, simple as that, can't do it in the water either, anyone can see that. So you have to be solidary and ready, always ready to stand your ground, and if there still is strength left in you, you energy bar filled with oats, nuts and valuable grains, you, a product yourself, we just can't see by whom or what kind, if there's still strength in you, then go ahead, help each other throwing us out, it is crucial for your social harmony and society's cohesion. We can understand that too. We can see that. You have seen it long ago. We can see it now too. It requires readiness for action and you've got it. No need to talk about it. Who would hear it anyway? Not even the waters of the Stygian swamp would hear us, and they hear everything, everyone who wants to get in and that's whom they hold on to. Here with you it's the other way around, you throw everyone out. The cow should also watch out not to step into the swamp; with the shoes she's wearing she won't get far. Won't make her curves more human, it says here, in this magazine.

We are many, but also just a few, we are the trickle that later runs out of freezer trucks, when we are finally frozen and then thaw again, smuggled, washed, no, not washed but spinning on the autobahn between those beautiful walls of your culture, always higher, always longer, for noise protection, not ours, that wouldn't have been necessary!, constructing walls we cannot see, wow, this car has walls all

around, can't look out, can't see a thing, nada, and yet there
are so many of us, and yet, we can't be seen either, they are
all ready to fight, but not for us, for—yes, it's written right
here—in this sacred book, I am God, your Lord, no, I am
your God, your Lord, no, it's not him either, you shall believe
in one God, yes, okay, but which one? There is one who has
us in his hands, who has our fall in his hands and probably
fells us himself. One. Okay. But we, we must spread ourselves, we must spread the Lord among many, for many
want to lord it over us and have us taken away, they want to
show us who is in charge, we never saw him, we are not
allowed to see him, how should we recognize him?, this car
has no side windows, so many want to show him to us, this
Lord, and that one there too; but there is only one, that one
Lord and that is the one they want to show us. How can he
be sufficient for all? What is he saying? Did you get what he
just said? I am the beginning who made heaven and earth,
yes, sorry, and the water too, of course! that's also needed,
we need it as a wet grave, that's what it is called by folks
headed for drowning, they'll make it!, oh well, peace is more
important than making, whatever it may be, that's our personal opinion, otherwise everything made will be hacked to
pulp again, it has happened to us, often in the countries we
come from, where they kill us, for he who makes shall also
unmake, everyone shall make and get rid of his own mess,
that's logical, even we can understand it, that we must be
gotten rid of, since we made ourselves come here, accusing
our Lord of harshness we dragged ourselves here, snuggled
together, yes, maybe also smuggled ourselves, to here, until
something carries us away again, maybe another flood,

which in the end turned out to be us, and often we even chilled ourselves in order to arrive fresh and ready to go, some didn't get up anymore, what for. But the State protects the rights, everywhere and everyone's, except ours. The State issues a ruling, but that rule does not apply to us, we do not belong to him, that precious State we had to apply to, but nothing applies to us. The public hand that protects and provides, we would bite into it, that is, we would bite it, if we'd ever get to see it, if it would make a contribution to our health in case we get moldy, expired, spoiled food on the alp, that sow, that sow of an alp, but sorry, we are in a church here, no, not anymore, there we also almost froze to death, like in the refrigerated car, but we did not defile your Lord, and we did not damage your healthcare system, we did not damage anyone and did not get anything, maybe we damaged a lawn, we only took what was offered to us, crap, crap, crap, but we were glad, well, more or less, after all it came from you, we complained, but we took the crap, that's all we got and we froze when the sighing wind drove through the pipes, not unlike whispered lamentations, but no warmth. Let's start all over again, it makes no sense for you to scream No!, we are starting again, and we won't get anywhere anyway: cohesion and cooperation from the basis to the top must exist, must persist, you insist, it's on this list, it already exists here, you insist on that, we are all for it, that is what distinguishes this republic, *wunderbar*, it is a wonderful country. Its water: also *wunderbar*! But we don't have that much of it, so we could not let great numbers of people in, that won't work, they'll have to go some place else if they want it so badly, if they want to get away at all costs. We, however, we however, hardly did we board reason, are drifting under water again, driven like animals, one following the other, but we don't want to follow any leader, we don't even know them, we don't know who is lord of the moment, no idea, doesn't matter, we however, we do not belong, we belong to no one, we belong nowhere, we don't belong to the community, we cannot contribute, we cannot pay the dues, we are responsible for ourselves, oh lord! We aren't even responsible for this fire-extinguisher, it isn't even here, what should we do if we were on fire, we couldn't extinguish it, it's already been tried many times, that nothing can be done about it and we are also irresponsible, because we did not find anyone else for it, you can't find someone irresponsible and someone responsible, who responds as such in a believable way is also hard to find; we would have been so happy, happy like a God about the newly invented art of singing and the innovative kidnapping of women, we would have really enjoyed it, we pay our dues every day, which consist of our own flesh, luckily not the meat we are given, you don't want to cut anything out of us, since there is nothing, can't squeeze blood out of a turnip, not even your government can cut it, so they cut to the chase, chasing us out, we are many, but we count little, we have nothing to count and no account, which creates little interest for the bank or in us, you, however, you can pay, you certainly proved it on a female, who fled from ungodly shame, a cow, no, that can't be right, so what!, she did flee from something, whatever, that Russian, who could get neither Opel nor the bank over here, that is, one could not move the other, the bank the Opel, not vice versa, well, sure, the Opel can't play games

with you, you drive it wherever you want and that's where
it wants to go too, but by then she was already a citizen, not
the bank, no, the sacred, glorious cow, with the help of that
man she became a citizen, I swear, she now is your fellow
citizen, she would have come anyway; her eyes touched
gently by the State's magic van and in an instant she was one
of yours, ready to get going, and you to get it on, in this
church, if necessary, exactly, just like that fabulous, perfectly
coiffed, perfectly tuned singer, exquisitely dressed, always,
expensively adorned, yes, that one does not need to serve as
tuning fork, her voice is a force of its own. No need to fork
her legs, no need to fuck anyone issuing her a short-term
visa, you must beg her, on your knees, for she comes with
the gift of this unique soprano voice, for which you've been
looking for so long, a voice to vote for, to make her come
more than once, no, what are you thinking, you won't find
something like that in your purse. Nothing can stop this
voice, it withstands any drugs, you can hear that, it just gets
stronger that way. No one has that kind of voice, no one gets
to voice it like her, there isn't any voice next to her and we
too get neither voice nor vote here. None whatsoever, not
even a weak one. We might have had a voice once, but now
it is gone, we almost had it, but nobody knows that, so we
don't get a second voice to the one we already have. No say,
no stay. Not one of us, no one in our crowd owns anymore
whatever he owns. No one has that voice, not even one. No
voice, no vote. We would like to but we don't have it; we
would like to use our voices for this land's common good,
altogether we would like to be useful to this land, which feels
comfortable inside itself, like a pig in shit or like that cow

who is no longer here, so we can't actually see what she is
doing, maybe she also wallows in shit, in good shit at any
rate, relaxing in some kind of light her passport brought her
under, she rests well, rests, she beams, she shines, and gets
turned off again, frolicking in the night that veils the hundred eyes, well, well, we never saw such general wellbeing,
we don't see it now either, she already left, she should have
been here at least for a short time, but now she is gone, who
knows?, maybe she stands right next to you, who knows?,
she shall be our role model and though she might have experienced terrible things, we don't believe it, well, yes, we are
not the only ones experiencing terrible things, we admit it,
oh, but could we just also be admitted, we want to be, oh,
so much, to belong here too, to you, well that's what you
thought right away, huh?, so you thought up something to
prevent that, even though we want it as much as that fantastic singer. Exactly as much, at least as much as her!, she has
the natural gift to—, no, not us, the daughter, her fellow
citizen, the daughter of the cow Europa—I still have to come
up with something for that one—but sorry to say, nothing
comes to mind, I should at least have Zeus—Jupiter as a
Roman and Io on my mind, and a gadfly, which was sent, sent
unlike us, we came voluntarily, yes a gadfly, a nasty bug or is
it buck?, stops us here, it does not admit us, the buck is to
blame, oh no, I am mixing up something again, the daughter,
whichever, seeing her dragged away as we do, by the precious
curls crowning her head, by her gown, by her grandiose
voice! No, I got totally lost here, lost even in this poor little
line, at least at the beginning, which will be like the end
anyway, I beg your pardon. Whatever I can accomplish

myself, I should do on my own the best I can, we can read
here, everyone can read it who knows how, but I can't, whatever it is, I can do nothing, I cannot possibly include all the
Greeks, the Egyptians, Europa, Io, not the big bug that keeps
us here and made us dig this hole, no, this mudhole, no, this
pit, this ground we break, out of bucks and without breaks,
I mean, brakes, we slammed on the brakes so hard that the
wheels dug into the ground, as we dug ourselves deep into
a hole, oh no, where can we get the twigs now, the olive
branches, whatever, to get going again, to set our fleet afloat
again, our little boat, wood would be best, so the radar won't
spot us, but that won't do us any good, we can see it already,
before it sees us; it won't help, our starry heavens will be
available soon, as per satellite radar, you can see the smallest
thing, the smallest wooden thing, oak veneer or laminate, a
paper boat?, no, plastic junk—same difference, we'll be seen,
we'll be seen! We'll be seen everywhere. We hide, but it
doesn't work, we duck, so the dolphin won't see us, the dear
little playful DOLPHIN, who is supposed to track us down,
to guard us, so that poor us cannot be put down and put out
by ground positioning systems, so that we can be detected
promptly and clearly on the open seas by Earth-observation
satellite-based systems, ouch, that could blow up in your
face, but not to worry, they monitor poor us, so that we can
be rescued in case of stupid accidents at sea. We only came
so he can locate us, whoever, so that he catches us, so he can
see us clearly, there must be someone who can look us in
the face, up there, who always optimizes the services in the
area of Border Surveillance, the combination of information
from cooperative positioning systems (VTS / AIS, VMS, and

LRIT) and remote-sensing observation systems (radar in particular), always successful. Never makes a mistake. Good thing we got them, good thing we got them all, yes, also the humming drones so that they guard us, observe us, keep watch over us, yes, that's it, so they watch over us on our way of all *being*? The sea has no sieve for our being, no strainer retains us when we must go down, no run-off grid, we just run off, just like that, there's no other way; after us, the ocean will instantly be smooth and even again, until the next ones are coming, or it tosses its curling waves, no, I won't say now it waved us in so we'd sink into its bottom, that would be too cheap, we have sunk low enough, we can't get any cheaper, but anything but the cheapest has not been available to us for a long time; never has been, no matter!, people are still cheaper, I am cheap enough to deal with them, you don't do that. You don't think we are such a deal and you don't want to deal with us, because we can't pay for ourselves and we don't have names and no one pays for us either. We do have names, but what are they good for? You don't want to know them and you are our yardstick. And you won't trade us for anything, no matter what. Our being has no currency, that's correct, we have been through many currents, but not on the exchange. We stand in the clearing of *being*, says the thinker, that Heidegg-man, no, say I, of water, which is clearing per se, which is a gigantic clearing, bounded by nothing but our death, that is to say our un-being, yes, one could put it that way, look at it that way; we crashed there, it was no party, currently we are swimming around in it, uninvited, among the sharks, not so swimmingly, but brazen, we have no choice, we are the uncalled for, the crashed, we will crush that shaky boat, the crooked one, yes, so many of us will not arrive to hack around in the clearing of being. We are the hacks in the endless clearing of un-being, stacked in the stocks of being and time, tiny holes in the infinite. What are we talking about? It's all according to the book. Come, have a look!

Children helping their mother in old age? An additional wife? No, thanks! No wife is enough. Even the cow was more than enough. Those guys also killed our mother, our brothers and sisters, our more distant relatives, furthermore, the most distant relatives, all of them, all, and they cut off the heads of our cousins and sent us the DVD of it, we already said that? We've said everything at least fifty times, give or take, yes, yes, I know, you can't take anymore, though you haven't heard anything yet. Again, we beg your pardon. We were and still are talking about mothers and children in old age, no, about children who never get to be old and their mothers who are dead, no, no, psychologically we have reached our limit and must get professional help, those are the employees of this church and now of the monastery, where you saw us lying on the floor, yes, nice people, help-ful, you can spread the word! Distribution of tasks and sup-port are important, not only in the family, which we don't have anymore, no wonder you call us irresponsible, parasites on your body that's ready any time to report freeloaders smearing their snot across this beautiful land, yes, us, they'll still report us when we're already down on the ground, they'll still report us just for being here, although we'd have responsibilities to our families, but all we have in terms of family is here, here with us, which is nothing, no one, nada and all we got is also nothing. Foreigners for foreigners. Measure for measure. Flashlight for night.

Precious curls, we've said it already several times, too many times, as always too many, doesn't matter, a fabulous soprano, she shows others than us who is wearing the pants, she shows Mister Putin, she puts on quite a show and tells Mr. Putin to show his pants; Mister Putin, show me what you've got, this goldilocks says, charmingly disarming papa bear, her teeth flashing, you'd think she might kill or blind you. Well, to see this woman dragged away by her dress!, we'd never want that, we couldn't even imagine it; seeing what happened to our mothers and sisters, we would never want to even imagine it happening to this incredible soprano, who produces sounds where the head rests on the neck, we talked about it before, we can't say it often enough and we can't imagine it either. This princess and that other princess, everything in Russian, by our command everyone goes Russian now, we all go for it, we go for the make of car and we get here in a car that functions, or only those who speak it go all the way with it, even in Kitzbühel, on the golf course, they can speak Russian everywhere, we can't even speak German, that's what they blame us for, with good reason, thank you for telling us again, we also say everything too many times and we don't know anything new. Those princesses know it naturally of course, Russian, that's all they need, even though many know a lot more, good for you, we are glad. Those two! Naturalized in a flash, they were naturals from the get go and so they got to be nationals. Please explain, but never mind, you already did, more than once: both are natural women, both natural-born winners, dressed to kill, and we have plenty more of them, in Kitzbühel, in Vienna, supplies everywhere in the world, even though there aren't hundreds of thousands like us, but they are wherever it's beautiful and there are many such places and those women are everywhere, maybe quite a few, especially conspicuous are their accompanying circumstances, I mean their Russian accompanists, no, not on the piano, their daughters' companions in the house on the busy, dusty lakeside road, no sign of life inside, she is not there, that woman, she'd never think of living in that shack, but at least no one's dead, we assure you, all alive, no lone ranger in the night here, everyone is elsewhere, no one ranging there either, the one trace of life here, us, is of no interest to anyone, no trace on the lake either, in the outlived house no one should live in anymore, on the contrary, it might collapse, who'd want to live there, well certainly not that one!, so then, she isn't dead, we guarantee you, you can bet our lives, how could she become a citizen?, alright then, we guarantee you no one died there, in that dump, not the daughter either, the European cow, excuse me, she turned into one only now, an official main residence has been registered here, which we don't have, she does, but she does not live there either, you are here to stay, you have a say, you have the voters, at least on your side, you have the sponsors but no trace of those—now I don't know myself whom I mean. Those others. Them. They are not where they are supposed to be, they are just gone, those Russians, yes, that's what they are called, they took off, probably as soon as they saw the house, no, they never saw it, they are bye-bye, it wasn't necessary anyway, they are gone and that's that. We are here, but then again we are not, we have nothing, but we aren't dead either. The distribution of tasks is important, life or death, everyone has to do his part, we can see that, it means some are dead, others are not, we are not, but many of us are, you might manage even more if you try really hard, for the State's distribution of tasks requires that you not be dead, we, however should be whenever possible, then we'll finally be gone or at least decimated, out of sight, out of mind, at any rate fewer than before, then there will be enough light, the bright light will be enough for more people, there will be enough for more when there will be fewer, that's obvious. We try, we are trying, a little patience, we beg you, this gadfly still bugs us, unfortunately, we can't move forward, we don't dare, that bugger's got a god's bite and that always draws the most blood, yes, you, good lord!, it's you we are talking about!

This house is empty, no corpses in there either, it has been rented, but stands empty. This flat above the supermarket, in Switzerland, is occupied, but also empty. Full and empty all at once. It seems to be a custom we don't yet know. Always ready to report, but no one lying there faint and pained whom one could look in the eye. But the hireling, what does God have to say about that?—can't look it up now, I don't have time, I have to write,—[*And I have to translate!*]—but the hireling—[*What is a 'hireling'?!*]—alright, I will look it up. 'The hireling, who is not a shepherd, and not the owner of the sheep, sees the wolf,' aha, *wunderbar*! the wolf comes in handy, [*oh now I see, a pun, punted in translation, hiring = renting in biblical German*], the hireling flees, because he just came for the money and does not guard the sheep, because he is a hireling, he does not care about the sheep, the foreigner does not care much for sheep, he might eat them and bury the bones next to his house, where unfortunately they will be found, but he does not care for them, sheep, no, not for the bones either, because he took on shepherding for pay. Nobody pays us, even though we would be happy to take good care of sheep, uh, no, of anything and anyone who wants our service! It's not really about service, not even about the rental, oh, how we wish that someone would rent, uh, hire us!

Well then, those in the house at the lake, those renting hirelings, those border-cruising boarders, then naturalized neo-nationals, naturalized, without ever having to show their deeply shadowed eyes, the Russian cow and the other one, I forgot her name, that one now also bought her home, just in time before it collapsed, yes the house, not she, I mean, seriously, are you living there or aren't you living yet?, what have they got, those women, that we don't? Is being women what they've got? Those could be men too, well, not the women, but men can come here too, then they would be businessmen, and they surely are coming, we cannot speak their names out loud, it would bring bad luck. The racer is now running at their expense, I mean, he drives, oh dear, not anymore and never again, he never spent time in a cockpit before, he never did time, still, the businessman shelled out for it all, the racer paid nothing, so now no one is driving anymore, and no one dwells in the stadium for suckers, I mean soccer, a game our suckers don't understand, they've got the ball constantly in front of their feet, but don't know what to do with it and so no one lives there anymore, he is alive, what, he kicked the bucket?, what a shame! If anyone should still be kicking, it's him and now all of a sudden, no more, his powerful hand dropped from the steering wheel, from the stick? Not even the driver races anymore? That's a shame, but now back to the question: How come they can and we cannot? They've got something and aren't here. We've got nothing and are here. And there are no receipts, though we lie here right in front of you, can't you see that?, well, there still are no receipts, no records of anything, because it's not about us, thus no need for any records, no records either of activities in that house, the one over there, the other house, we are not talking of the house of God, of course, no record of the daughter stopping for a moment in her main residence, which she needs, which we don't have, nothing could ever stop that one! No one knows her, not even the landlord, no one knows her, no one knows any names, pardon me, her name is known, it's ours that isn't, no one knows our names, back home everyone is dead and now here too, what a mess, a real bummer! No one knows us anymore, that doesn't speak for us at all, not even a little, because we are the last to speak, we are not the ones who get the last laugh. The daughter has a voice to speak for her, she isn't here, but a voice speaks for her and she also gets to vote; it comes with her voice. She can't be seen but she's got a voice that makes her an instant citizen, with all the rights and duties to promote and demote the general welfare, sorry, wrong constitution, but if you are a woman and pretty, everything is easier right away, which must feel pretty good, but not to us and I don't even know right now what feeling I mean, we promote all freedoms, though not for free, but any contribution, however much, I said it before, and with pleasure, because it says so right here, is valuable for our fellow human beings, even if you can't see them, valuable for the common good, even if it doesn't do any good, like in this community, even if we are not commonly referred to as a community, it's all valuable, it enriches everything, everybody enriches himself, sure, this voice has been bought and that vote too, it is now among us, one of many, but one that counts!, it liveth among us, she hath lived among us, but she hasn't been seen, now she lives above us in a loft, but she still can't be seen. But she can vote, she has a voice, she's always had her voice, the voice, right!, she got it all, but doesn't all flesh have an expiration date, like the grass in front of the church? Now look, this woman has even two, a voice and a vote, but no decay, she just got it all. She got it right. I said it right. Because joining is better than watching.

We chose a church and then a church chose us, so now this is the place we stay for real, feel free to come and take a look, we could also be staying some other place, we have options. We could stay at the bottom of the sea, in the water, in the desert, without water for a change. Our experiences will be sent to us in time to have them while we are having them and then they will have become superfluous. We don't need them anymore. Let alone in water, forget experience, it is totally superfluous! You might not be able to still come today, and we might once again not even be staying here anymore. We were not used to having a place to stay and now we are living here for a bit, which interests no one, we are the forgotten, no one knows us anymore after we showed up here, they took us in and now we are out, out of the church, that's the main thing, we all worked on that, it took some wrangling by quite a few and they pushed it through!, and we don't have a phony residence in some house either, let alone a phony flat in Switzerland, what are you thinking!, we said we did, but we don't live there, God lives there, the new lord and master, the citizenmaker, automobile mover and shaker, deal faker and breaker, who likes tightening screws, but whatever he does: it's shaky, and we know it. He lives on heavily trafficked thoroughfares, but that's not where he lives, of course, he doesn't live above supermarkets with thousands of people and goods inside, all without him, pity on them!, they might feel orphaned without him, who knows, but no, he certainly doesn't live there, everything empty, house empty, address full, here it says full address in Switzerland, residence in Switzerland, Canton Zug, done, filed and saved, naturalized, from the secured residence into security, top security that is, not one hair on his still full head gets hurt or torn out there, because never has anyone seen anyone there, but this citizen is a natural, like in his natural habitat which he inhabits sight unseen like any other inhabitant there, for that's the habit there, and it all goes so fast, no one dwells on it, dwelling somewhere one is not, we think that in principle everybody there is a naturalized, sorry we mean, a natural inhabitant, because even he cannot be naturalized thrice; he who dwells is the monocot, I mean monogod times three, three in one, who would embrace a morass, unfortunately we don't remember what we meant by "morass," surely not what it means to you; who would disappear there?, who can be here as well as not be here?, no records of a reviewing process, only the woman has been naturalized, yes, indeed, the Russian, a not-quite-legally legalized, free citizen, if not for free, even a dual citizen, two is better than one, organized by the company god father, who now has organized a party, his own political party, why not, he has a ball, he's on the ball, somebody has to be the kicker, even we, the living dead still must be kicked around, into the church, into the monastery, into the balls, no matter, there must be a kick in it for everyone, the heavenly goalie hangs on the wall, but the ball is still in the game. We, however, want to know who calls the shots, not of schnapps, the boss!, and the answer is already coming in, because everything gets divided up, the way people were sent everywhere to spread the word of God, because they did not have their own, just as people are distributed to all countries, just as this country is split up into nine states, his people also have their fields of work, where they can reap big profits or not, it is completely up to them, they are down on us, but up to getting rich or not. They have every right and every responsibility; they've got it all, because their special qualities and skills are paid attention to. They don't know ours, maybe we also have skills, we don't know ourselves. We are blinded by them and troubled by us, because our skills sprout somewhere else where we have no access to them. We are not still, but no one wants to hear us. If you hesitate to set up camp all alone you can always bed down some other place. You have the choice. No god sticks the heavenly scepter in your face: this far and no further, he does not reside where we looked him up. We looked for him, on the map, with the GPS, with the route planner, which can calculate even the walking time between trains, depending on how you walk, slow, medium or fast, and you keep going and going or swimming and swimming, you drive and drive, you are sinking and you are almost all the way down, and you are rescued, no, you are dead! Not rescued. Depends what you are, if a No is your fate and no more procedure needed, then all processing, any proceedings would be superfluous like the water above you, the answer is no. You are looking for the lord your master, but he is not where you are looking for him, the invincible master, who is the city, the people, who is everything, he calls the altar his, the hearth of the land, okay, okay, we do not doubt it, it's just that where the letterhead says he is, he is not, not resident, not visiting, not visionary, we can attest to that meanwhile. We are stuck in the Nowhere and that god's stupid fly still keeps us there, it stings and stings and Europa pops out, no, I still have to look that up, it was entirely different, we could tell you, were we not rolling in the mud so lazily. Why don't you tell us!, you won't?, even though you could google it like anyone else, if you had the device for it, which you do, oh yes, you do. In the ocean you don't need a GPS, no one has a clue there, not even a machine, wrong, only machines do!, no one else, the ocean is too big for you? We could have told you so right away. We know from our own experience. It simply is too big. Can't see the end. We know, we've been there, close to the end. It did not support us, the sea. No wonder, it does not have any supporting structures either, no, no foundation, what for, for us it is bottomless anyway. It is as everything is. It has been laid down where building is permitted, because the land knows best whom it can count on and whom it can build on. And it does, because it is important to create living spaces. Eating is important too, but we don't want to ask for too much. We are tired, we went as far as the capital, we lied down in a church, our few belongings, our donated junk, our crap, which is us too, which we are supposed to clean up, at least part of that pitiful crap was pushed together by a bulldozer in a few seconds, done, finished. We did not have to do anymore. We did not have to help. All over.

No more area of activity to be filled. No more area the area manager admits us to. We are the ones to admit: Every person is illegal. That is true. Every one of us. No insurance we could trust. No assurance we would believe, no regional specialty we could taste, no influences which could lead to diversity, well, you prevent that, of course, no unique diversity and no small individual unit. That's what we could be in a pinch, yes, we could, exactly, we could do our duty, but you don't see that at all, no task that could be accomplished, possibly by us, but you don't care, no distribution of tasks, and so we can't take on, over or under anything. In contrast to you and your connection, I can't think now of the lady's name, Europa, no, Io, I, from the South, the *Südländer*, well, it is I, just I, but that is not enough, my name is not enough. Poor me, she says, bugged and impregnated, not guarded by a god, but goaded by a gadfly, no, wrong, that God impregnates everyone but me, not the cow, what would be the outcome! We'd rather come in than out, but that is a no go. Out you go, not in. You hear noise and arguing from the apartment next to you? There is a conflict? We come and that is what we do, we make noise, we argue, we create the conflict, we do that easily. For you can always call for help, the police are always there for you. Not for us, not for us. For us too, but in another way. From the other side they are here for us, they already managed to break through to us, they kicked in the door, the water pushed right through, they stepped right through the water, well, it's not solid, no harm done. Through various exchanges we found out that the police were there for us, they came especially for us. Only to get us out and avoid panic. To intervene ourselves is *verboten*. No intervention for us. We are the ones to be prevented, the ones picked out, padded down or just picked over on the fly, just in case, okay, here's the fly, go for it. If you find something, keep it. We are not allowed to, here comes the bulldozer! This rickety table was a donation! It's not ours! The dozer doesn't give a damn. Don't stay out of this conflict out of fear, which one?, that one, right here!, grab the opportunity, grab what you can! It'll be worth it for you. If you see someone in need, take heart and do something! If you see us, grab us! Size us up, seize us and provide security, a little bit of security for your state, your fellow citizens, your neighbors, throw us out. Remove us like a grease stain. Remove us, do away with us! Save yourself from us! Yes, that's good. It's the only way for a society where human rights are raided, raked up, thrown on a pile and run over by a bulldozer, I mean, where rights are respected, especially that one farthest to the right. What? Forget it. I mean one society of course, it first has to become one. That's what you want, don't you? Becoming one with you and with itself, then you won't have to flee, across deserts and over the mountains. We just aren't a society, or just a small one, meaning not yet, maybe that has something to do with the hired shepherd, who does not belong to his herd, who was just hired? And hired just for animals? We are just a lot, not as many as the animals, but quite a few, at least some, but not a society and this is the only way to create a secure society: by removing us. Just get us out! We are thinking how we were discovered to begin with, it was dogs who found us, the shepherd's dogs, the loyal helpers. Now you help too! Our things have been thrown out already, we don't mind following them, like we follow you too, your orders, we are gone! Get rid of us. You must assure the security of the land, the police have to too, you see, that makes already two, take care of security and get us out. However you proceed, proceeding or no proceedings, whatever, chase us away! Get us out! Whatever the outcome of the proceeding against us, drive us out! Or just let us glide into the water! Yes, where we are right now. Let go of us, no big deal, and off we go. Or not? Let's leave together for once, that would be kind of nice, why don't you flee with us!, but no, you wouldn't want to, you want to drive off, but not like that, no, not like you can't imagine from where. Our spirit perturbed you, strange, we don't even have any, our lawn- and law-abusing feet, we forgot all about it, no, we didn't, we did—several times, probably too many times, at least a hundred people had called—we did report that now the grass in front of the church is all gone too, flattened, ruined, kicked into the dust, for good. And it had just been freshly seeded last spring, only so the dust can settle on it now, our donated belongings removed by the bagger, all gone, our gross human malformations are not a sight for you to behold, our bodies, half-animal, half-human, like that Europa or Io, well, which one of the two is it now, half-maiden, half-cow, gazed at in wonder for millennia, people don't do that anymore, but they do love to stare, in peace and quiet, because the Atlantic god sits next to them, no, not the Atlantic, we don't need that big an ocean, a small one will do! That's plenty for all of us, promises this god and he protects them, his speeches save the day and take life out of us. You want us gone? You bet, right now! Out! Oh, God, who takes pity on ours, on us, unfortunates, driven to madness, right into madness, half-animal, half-human, not human at all, nothing at all, who takes pity on us? Do you also want to draw a lot and show some feeling perhaps? You don't want to? We understand.

The daughter, the shame-free maiden, no, that she definitely is not, in that house, in the deserted house, legalized, naturally, hush, hush, in a flash and a crash, the Russian occupant, never seen, unknown, but us you can see, you can come and see us any time you want to, but you don't want to. We are not value, we are extraneous to the values produced by others, promoted by the corporation, set in motion by the concern, by the daughter's naturalization, the one who sings in concerts, no, we mean the other one, who can't do anything, but maybe that's a prejudice, we have already been judged, so why not some prejudice for others? We always have some left, no problem, no harm done. The Opel firm has not been bought, though that man certainly wanted to buy it, the parent company prevented it, the corporation, the endless eternal times' ruler over all of us did not release him, God, our lord, was not released from his divine breath, he still is needed, needed to start a whole party, if he is not allowed to build whole cars, he, the supplier, the go-between, but the goners are always us; this plant, the corporation's pawn, God's pawn, a god greater than God, there is always a greater one, greater even than any god—and the desire for MORE, people's best desire, the one that makes something of them, well, not of us, but of all the others— this pawn of God to make more of oneself, the one carried carefully in the womb, like Io carried Europa, unlike the sea that didn't want to carry us, unfortunately, it just didn't want to, neither did the boat, what can you do about that?, we are doing nothing, the boat does not carry us, it does not care for us, the sea doesn't carry us either, we rise in it like dough, our fat swells, if no one comes right away we will be hidden forever like Io and Europa, it's high time, and the two don't even exist!, never did!, just as well!, what doesn't exist can't get lost, something like that, not even close, I am sure—so something is conceived, something gets constructed, which unfortunately was not allowed to be constructed or it got lost before it was conceived, or broken up in parts and shared, as common stock, but not with us. So nothing comes of it. No cars. And cars are the highest of anything, the boat the lowest, but necessary nonetheless, also for us. It just didn't do us any good. Our stuff, our junk is gone, our donated things pushed together, broken and taken away, only we are left and now all around the land is cheering and telling the truth, word of honor, though they wouldn't have to tell, we knew it anyway, but they do tell nevertheless.

We cannot be the sons of that god, it must be others, we don't know who, we are to get lost, perhaps not killed, but out for good, good. This house can boast: They are finally gone, and I've had enough too, don't thank me, no need for it. Maybe you don't feel like coming anymore either, crashing through the door, blasting a hole through the wall, denting the ocean, if only in passing, but without a pass, throwing teargas, shedding tears, getting rid of all the junk, don't feel like it anymore, just don't want to anymore, for all the good intentions went into the plant and many have been naturalized by now; Yeltsin's daughter transplanted, great!, we didn't think it would work, but sadly, it won't do us any good! The firm naturalized, the bank already here, bank at hand or no naturalizing. But it didn't work out. Doesn't matter. Well, maybe not to you, we don't doubt that, but maybe it does to the gentlemen from the firm. So then, this naturalization has already happened, too soon, but done is done, it didn't get us anything, a bad investment, naturalizing Yeltsin's daughter a job well done, there she lies, nature surrounds her, no beasts, no hunters dare to come near her, no, not here, she must be elsewhere, she must be lying elsewhere, we don't know where, the curtain is closed, the insights gained narrowly defined, adding up to only a few pages, who'd write about that, who'd sing about that, who does what, who acts how, who forces the folks here and their daze-crazed smiles, dazed from the bull they concocted for us, who forces them to join the other dead victims, we would have also fit right in with them, well, maybe not all that well, but still? Never mind. Pay no mind. We set the horizon for something that could end happily too, but doesn't. We set up nothing, we upset no one, we are dead anyway, at least we look like it. And it says so right here, no, it doesn't, not right here, that the dead can also be naturalized, no, and there's nothing about the living dead either, nothing said about the living dead, nothing, nothing about those whose dead are still so much alive and whose living are dead, none of that, we don't want to hear it. The last one does not see the light, he turned it off. And the last thing is us.

Yet, it's not our fault. We have respect, we show respect, we like respect and here it comes, we want it to meet ours right away, they meet halfway, but ours is not accepted, we cannot pay respect, we bring different talents and strengths, but, unfortunately, no money, and those don't get accepted. Nothing gets accepted, at least not when it comes from us. They only take from us. The bulldozer takes care of that. We are not accepted, in our case the word does not have to stand for any firm or work for us, we have to walk their talk and rather fast, the firm stands firmly on its own, it doesn't belong to anyone, certainly not to us; whatever we did, before, is now in secret darkness, and there is no one anymore to lift us in his mighty hands. Because we do not offer a Russian bank, we do not crank up the car industry, we don't even crank up cars, we keep our foot always on the brake, we can't let go of it, otherwise we would be stuck in nowhere, on the contrary, we might actually be driving, but we have dug ourselves too deeply into your mother soil, that bug—no, not the car—the gadfly has put the brakes on us, otherwise we would not stand here, we would be driving, don't flee from us; we would flee ourselves if we could. We have no merit and no earnings, we also have weaknesses, that's all we have, we do not and never will have citizenship, and we don't have anyone's sponsorship, the only ship we had was an old, sinking boat, we have nothing, no one speaks for us and we don't speak either, nor do our dead speak, least of all for us, like our deeds, they might speak, but not for us, how could they, they are far away, our deeds and our dead are far away, can't go any further, they had their heads cut off, no, not their deeds, that recently happened to my cousins, not quite by accident it was captured on video, nowadays everything comes with a video or a picture. The Russian princess wasn't stopped anywhere, not in her house on the much trafficked road in the borderland region, she is, after all, a citizen now, nobody saw her, maybe she doesn't exist, no, she must, for she is a citizen now, the *Herr* God made it happen, for he rules with almighty power, the highest of all and he does not look up humbly to anyone above him, only his values look at him, and his valves, bolts, brakes, exhausts and other body parts, from valves to values, but they don't belong to anyone, not even the good lord, yes, that one who wanted to create values got them, sure, whatever sprouts in his mind is a done deed in a flash, no, not this time, pity!

We have not been set up by anyone, we are just here, just so, all others dead, we'll soon be too, you'll see, don't hesitate to celebrate too soon, although there is time, plenty of time to celebrate later, for he who laughs last must really have something to laugh about. And when we are gone, you can rejoice and rejoice some more that we are gone, that you could solve this conflict without force, because another force solved it in your name, which you don't want to admit. We would like to take on this task, but around here there always is—and we really mean: always—some deputy putting in a day's work before putting on the green, putting his foot down when it comes to the rights of others, smashing the donated folding table with the plastic cups, squashing the camping chairs, also donated, trashing and removing our few belongings, which aren't even ours, the bagger takes care of it—makes it easier for you, and even though those aren't living things: this is lived civil courage, even though you might have to fear disadvantages on account of it. But you don't, you don't have to fear anything, let alone disadvantages, you have nothing to be afraid of, come on in, please, and trample down everything, it has a short-term effect, which you can easily extend by crushing us as well, we are not even as hard as this wobbly plastic table, not as hard as this outdoor furniture, for which someone somewhere had no more use, because it had already been used too long. If all of us did that, if all of us did all of that, we'd live in a safe country, well, safe from us at least, that's something. The existential possibilities of coexistence, we said it already, we are saying it again in case you didn't get it, require indisputably that one can step on, no, step in for another. But of course you don't want us to step in for you, you don't even want us to step out to stretch our legs in front of the church, that would ruin the beautiful lawn even more, and more every time, we already said it because you said it, the lawn that had just been freshly seeded (who said: last spring?), like a mother's womb because—listen now: stepping out into the world, stepping up the manifold ways of being-in-the-world, we've said it before, but it's so much fun, is not limited to the polished possibilities of public being-together-ness, it equally pertains to those in restricted spaces, with restricted possibilities, us, yes, it pertains to us too, because we too are possible, even though you don't believe it, we are human, after all, we are also others, we might be some of the ones and some of the others, we also have professions, no, not anymore, status, states, no, we have no more states, how could we, states of mind, yes, we have that, so then, the possibilities tailored to all of this, the possibilities of—what is the word?—*besorgen*, taking care of, what about it? oh, yes, it pertains to everything I just mentioned, period; it pertains and applies to . . . Take your pick! This sentence never ends, it isn't mine, it's by that Heidegghead, just as your power never ends, which comes from you and returns to you, which knows where it belongs, caution, high voltage!, here it comes! Please step back from the edge.

We pay respect to others fair and square as is required from us, we shall treat others as we want to be treated our-selves. And this is what we do, we pay respect, it even tries to get ahead of us and pay in advance, respect, but it is out of cash, so it pays more attention to us, which suits our intention, as we intend to pay it something, we will pay its dues one more time, we pay it more respect even though we already paid our dues more than once, we can't remember the last time, but we got something for it, I think it was a thermos because it was so cold in the church, and that is exactly how we want to be treated, that is how we want to be treated ourselves, not like the Russian President's daugh-ter, she does not need respect but gets it all, we on the other

hand pay open-handedly and with an open heart, we came
with respect, where shall we put it, we took heart and
brought you respect, since we got some too, where shall we
lay it down, the respect? And where can we lie down ourselves then? Respect spread out too much. There is no more
room. Should we put it next to our talents and strengths, so
we have it at hand whenever we want to fall back on our talents and strengths, so it will lie right there as well, the respect
we got, or not? Well, we did not steal it! Honestly. We paid.
Respect. Indeed. We paid for it. So, let's do it, let's do it now.
Right now. Let's get respect and fairness together, yes, our
talents and strengths, which are lying there next to each
other, already laid to rest, we wanted to have our hands free,
we don't need them here, we don't need those things, that
camping table, we could have used it, sometimes folks want
to hang with each other, right?, but that's collapsed now, no
one needs them here, fairness, no, or respect, or us, but
maybe it'll pay off. We'll put it together, okay, here we go,
everything together, it takes up less room that way. Let's pile
up everything we have, maybe we can buy something with
it? Let's hope so! I hope they let us in wherever we are supposed to be, added to all those other Dicks and Toms and
Harrys who we are supposed to be too. But we cannot be.
We can't. We put together what we have and there is the
bulldozer, still dozing in the icy cold in front of the church,
in the frozen grass, frozen as well, all of us frozen, though
inside, in the house of God, then everything will be done
away with. All done and gone. We wanted to dwell in this
kingdom, but we don't have permission. Having a home,
leak-proof and quiet, with the others would be nice, but you

don't like it. No small houses ready for us to move into, only this monastery, we can stay here because we can be thrown out again any time, maybe we have been already, since getting thrown out means staying for us, just elsewhere, and yes, we still are at your service, just say the word, use your voice, vote, maybe even for us! Be selective! What else are elections for? You don't want to give us shelter. So now all the citizens who decided to get us out of their sight, to cast us out, are going to cast their vote, for their own God and good; their scale in delicate balance, the parties look at us, they want to be just, no, they don't, and anyway, no one does us justice either. So, are you now expecting better friends than us? What do you expect? Better than us? Not shame would we have brought you, we would have taken on the shame, would have felt ashamed whenever you wanted us to, as for those in need of protection every word said quickly adds up to a sentence when rumors run wild and turn into hate. That's how it goes. That's how it is. We warned you, we would have tried, we would have lamented our difficult lot, and we would have tried very hard, we promised we would try hard, we just didn't know what, why and what for, we do what we can, we would not have hurt, not even touched any creature or man, that does not belong to us, but we may not belong to you, you beware of us. You tolerate everything, it is only us you don't. You do not avoid insult, we served our foes' lust and scorn, we would have liked to avoid that, believe us, it was not possible. Forgive us. Housing we would have liked available to us, whatever the city would have wanted to give us. Burdens and duties would we have gladly accepted. Whatever advice father state would have given us, we would have preserved it, faithfully, in good faith, for shyness and modesty mean more to us than our lives, which we can't lead anyway. Okay. And now we'll be happy to also praise something, yes, your god too, we've been in his house after all, it looked nice, all cleaned up, at least until we crashed there and got pneumonia and several hunger strikes. We praise the city, may it never be flooded, it won't happen, it does not have an ocean, there is a stream, the current is strong, it generates a lot of power, the city is prepared, it has its own power grid and a floodplain, maybe even more grids and power plants, but it has only one in power, unfortunately we do not know him. He did not come, he did not have to, he was already here. There is a plan for everything, just not for us. Okay, we can understand that, you couldn't have known that we would come, we made no reservations, though you have many, we arrived unannounced. We are the unannounced. The supplicants. The nailed ones. No, we wouldn't let you go that far. You have your god who is up to that, but not us. Not many look with pity on us. Others lord it over us from up high and don't see us, even though they are right above us, they should be able to, even from an airplane, even as an eagle. But no! They turn away, they look another way, but with keen eyes, as always. The lust for hunting is stronger, it gets ever stronger, but they don't see us, the scale tips, it sinks with us, we were taken out of the icebox, the hunt was over long ago, so there we lie, a few pieces of flesh and it is happening now, maybe it has already happened by the time you see this, what fate dealt us, that is, the end. The disappearance. The turning away from us, on both sides, turning to one side and then to the other. It keeps us in motion. Okay. Unmoved are those who are easily moved, moved by cat videos, moved by puppies, still veiled the future approaches us, yet even veiled we can see it, we already got to the bottom of rock bottom, wasn't so bad, we had no grounds for it, while even the ocean has one, somewhere, we just wanted to take a look, yes, we can already see the future, yes, that one, over there, in the still more secret past, tell us what we should still beg for and most of all, why? Whom? That justice will be done to us, we pray for that, may it be the fulfillment of my prayer for safe conduct, for a better lot. But it will not happen. It will not be. It is not. We are not here at all. We came, but we are not here at all.

Aeschylus: The Supplicants

Ministry of the Interior, State Secretariat for Integration

Ovid: Metamorphoses

And a pinch of Heidegger, a must, can't do without it.

SCENES OF TRANSLATION
Notes on *Coda* and *Appendix*

After I finished translating *Charges* the refugee crisis in
Europe quickly escalated into one of the biggest forced
migrations in European history since World War II
with scores of refugees—mostly from the Middle East,
Afghanistan, Pakistan and Africa trying to escape civil
wars, terror and persecution—arriving everyday. For
example, in 2015 Germany alone took in more than a million refugees. In her characteristic open dramaturgy
Jelinek responds to the burgeoning crisis with addenda to
the main text, similar to what she did with her earlier play
The Merchant's Contracts (2015). A keen, compassionate
observer of local and world events, she wrote the two
brief sequels to *Charges* between September and October
2015.

The *Appendix* was triggered by the Hungarian government's closing of the borders to Serbia, which resulted in
a situation where massive floods of refugees were fenced
in under shockingly inhumane conditions. Coincidentally,
at the same time international media broke the scandal
that the Volkswagen Group violated various anti-
pollution acts, which mandate emission levels for diesel
cars. Always quick to respond to disturbing topical events,
Jelinek interweaves these events, which she experienced
mainly via media coverage, with similar tragedies echoed
in canonical literature.

Coda reflects the contemporary refugees' voyage in 'splinters', the term she uses in the concluding quasi-bibliographical list of references—passages from the *Odyssey*, Euripides's *Iphigenia in Aulis* and Ezra Pound's variations on Homer in *Cantos*. For the latter she cites the most recent translation by Eva Hesse published in 2012. The quotes from the *Odyssey* are clearly from the canonic translation by the eminent German translator, philologist and poet, Johann Heinrich Voss (1751–1826). True to her sources, the opening lines of *Coda* set the scene as a translation—the writer struggling to find the right German word for "tremble" (*zittern*). "Something's trembling, it is trembling, isn't it, the boat, no there's another word for it, no that won't nail it either, it wobbles, the boat, it shakes, probably because Hermes and Athena are not installed as shaft of compass as something trembling between them," obliquely refers to Pound's Canto 7: "Gods, / Hermes and Athene, / As shaft of compass, / Between them, trembled— . . . " References to attempts of finding "the right term" are woven throughout the text.

Homebound due to agoraphobia, Jelinek experiences reality as translated by the media, triggering a series of eclectic literary associations. She acknowledges 'a pinch of Freud' in the *Appendix*; the 'pinch' both deliberately and literally gets out of hand to become 'oversalted' like the (sea) water referred to in *Coda*. Freud's analysis of the child's anal stage translates into Jelinek's anal humor which is her translation of the everyday crisis faced by the refugees—the absence of sanitary facilities in their camps—an absurd situation that is also employed by several xenophobic governments to induce fear in their citizens. It is the lived experience of the trauma that ultimately makes it impossible for a writer, or anyone who is not a refugee, to translate the enormity of the global refugee crisis.

CODA

Something's trembling, the boat, it is trembling, isn't it?, no, there's another word for it, no, that won't nail it either, it wobbles, the boat, it shakes, probably because Hermes and Athena are not installed as shafts of the compass, something is trembling between them, the boat trembles from fear, no it rocks because those people can't sit still; no one is holding the sails, it doesn't have sails, well they would come in handy, it still has air, the boat, and it will need it too, some air is still in it, but not for long. There still is air above, but not for long. Then it'll go downward, and then we'll take a bath. The body becomes thought becomes body, and the thought relates to its host like the edge to the knife. Is this the way to the marble forest with the stone trees, if so, we would like to be here, no this is the way to Greece, to the gods, you might never get there, you and your buddies, I mean this boat is like—now I can't think of the word, like a densely covered pincushion in the women's world, I don't want to say full, yes but full it is nonetheless. No pine forest nearby, the boat avoided it, the water is denser than glass but unbreakable—parting, merging—what belongs together flows together, all one, all the same, water. Only people, those who fall in, go kaput. They don't break, the water takes them in, it opens its trap, no, can't say trap, just as one can't say tremble, could somebody please hand me new words, many thanks, words are on the march, some have been written down here too, the kitchen is open, only there's nothing to eat, no, nothing to drink either, isn't that enough water for you here, you really want more?, but that one is so salty, it's clearly oversalted, can I send it back?, yes, it goes back but then it won't come again, let alone improved, that's not how we meant it. Calm down, you can drink it okay, you can drink up a storm but you can't scream while you are drinking, obviously. Silver floods of light above the waves, you've got to see that. I haven't seen it in a long time. The lament emerges from the dark, hell casts shadows, for there is light from the fire, the flames strive seawards, the people converge in the ocean's claws. Copper glow, gleam of waves drift under hulls at night, under the ships' bellies? But this ship has no belly, we are its belly, without us it would be a rubber rag, and if it were a belly, a few hundred would immediately drown, they'd drown on the spot, no, thank you, I hope this belly has eaten already, thank you, it did, it keeps the food inside, look here, there's air in it, I'd say it consists of air, it's an airliner but not in the clouds. Air is lighter than water, it just can't swim on its own, it needs a case, air does, a husk, which can be thrown out as needed. Every boat must be destroyed after use, I find that excessive, that's like pounding screws with a hammer into the water where they won't stick. The air in the boat is sometimes surrounded by people who have been breathing it, or by rubber if it's a rubber raft, which consists of air with a thin layer, the so-called top layer, so that the air can't escape, so it won't come out, sure you can do it, who is keeping you? What happens afterwards is proof of a sense for fine differences—some know how to swim, others don't. Fate. But, know-how is also part of it. Out with you, it's only water, you can't be afraid of that, most of the earth's surface consists of it, and without water you would die, in it too; nevertheless, at least you'd still have a chance there! I ask you, you aren't really afraid of water, are you? That would be a contemptible gift handed to you, fear is a contemptuous gift, fear likes contempt, it looks down on you and laughs its head off so you can keep it.

It is night now, no just a moment, don't be hasty—not yet. The drift pulls away below the boat's belly. This boat plays into the hands of the storm, even if it doesn't stretch its hands, it falls right into it, storm's hands are the boat's home, it whirls itself into them and ventures even further, into ashen greyness, into thick blackness when it's night or when the dark is deep enough, no ice weighing down its hull, this is a southern ocean—please pay attention to the zone of this water, please also pay attention to its owners—and yet around the heads nothing but the dense blackness we can't use for anything else later, therefore the word dense and the word black. The night is wide open, yes and happily so, even for this boat, it makes no difference to the night, no, we travel by day, no night, no blackness, that's below the water during the day, and at night anyway, if you absolutely want to get in there you will see it, the blackness, the impenetrable, which looks sort of blue on the outside, is this even blue, or is it AdBlue?, you can google it, if you aren't driving a modern diesel including its nitric toxics, but you don't have to. Over there, on the other hand, people suffocate because they've got nothing to breathe in, I can't really see it clearly, I am sitting in a chair, looking at the photo of a poultry transporter and there's a lot more on YouTube; several groups, even this boat could carry those, not me, I can't swim.

The water doesn't knock me out, I am high and dry, that's where I belong, it doesn't matter there if something knocks me out, but in the ocean, the water always only knocks over a boat on which I am not, I can't swim, so why would I get on a boat!, and now the boat can't swim anymore either anyway, I would not find it even if it scattered seeds along its way. Yes, the sea is wide open below the boat, come on in if you've bought a ticket, you've paid for the whole package—yes we are open, but that's the wrong ticket, it's not valid here, there it says passage from country to country but not which one—but we are not in the country and not in the city either, not in a city of our choice, not in a city we were assigned to, but neither are we waved through, no one catches us, no light to serve as a lasso, so then I sink, by morning I am sinking, says the sea spitting out its gum which could not improve its breath, sometimes I too have to eat something, says the sea. I can do whatever I want. The black-eyed beast Sea can simply do whatever it wants. Darkness is not only in the eyes, we also make the dark, so we can make it inside it, so we can ride on it, on the raft, on the river, in every water. The flesh is aglow in the dark, it has devoured the glowing ball, and what do we see now, what are we supposed to see now? Could it be railroad tracks we are seeing here?

Dark shoulders that triggered the lightning, that man in the swim trunks shows off for starters, though he doesn't take much time for it, how the motor works, no he doesn't want to come along, what for?, he's got his money alright, the young man, good body, he must swim a lot, good for the waistline, the ideal line, which he does not have to sail himself, he is lucky, that God, who is in control of the motor and also shows it to others, he knows the motor as he knows what's locked up in his swim trunks, still he must leave it now, he won't see it again, the motor will take off, the people have been loaded in, they're led on and if they don't like it they'll just have to transfer the forest to here. If they want shade, the forest will have to come here. So you'll just have to pull or tear at something here, throttle there, then threaten, then stop again, I don't know whatever it is a motor does when it works. But the fuel has been put in, it's the stuff that gets us going, the motor has ingested the fire, it snarls and now it's running, though spluttering right from the start, it's spitting at us, something's not right here. Why shouldn't it work, why not, after all it was fed with this good diesel so that it keeps warm, no, not watered, only fuelled, why shouldn't it run further than us who've got no fuel at all, for what fuels us is inside us, at least we have it right on hand there. Something is wrong here. Something is wrong with this motor. This is no motor, this is no branch, those are not tracks, those are not clouds, this is something that roars and spits, no berries ripen near it that's for sure, why am I saying this? Because someone else said it before me though not in front of me but I am on the safe side with him unlike this boat. The dolphin man, the supposed savior-hero, butterflies back to the shore, soon he'll be high and dry, he lets the boat take off by itself, it knows what it has to do, the people finally got the idea too, they know now how the motor works, they had an introductory course at a bargain rate, which the ocean is spared, it doesn't need a rate when something is imported. The others have to stay the course. The boat swims in the water like birds on the tips of trees, but that isn't swimming, they can get off any time, those lucky ducks! You are now on your own, ladies and gentlemen, I would like that too, I don't even own myself, I am the ship but not the owner, who just jumped ship and left me a wreck. Hey you, Water, can you give me a way-leave? Else there's no way for me to find my way across, all on my own. Someone would have to put me there. All alone. Just like a mountain, enveloped by the breath of life, enveloped by what?, no idea, but there are no mountains here, there is only the sea, there is the Lite, people dance on it like birds on the tips of trees, no, they are not dancing, they are barely kicking, at least not yet the bucket, they keep still, and don't move,—just don't move! The birds would rather go on foot than into the water, they know what to do, sitting down where bough is bent over bough, look, that crow would also like a piece of bread, like the one I am about to throw there, but now it's fallen in the water, where the crow can't land. The water isn't the land, there, there is the way to Naxos, to Lesbos, to Kos or wherever, where I have never been—it's a straight line but not to there—come along, guys! Yes, the children too. Come along but not that way! Ay, that way, that way leads there if we come along. Take a look over the bow, what do you see? You can't steer the ship eastward to Kythera or wherever—you won't be able to if the noise puts you to sleep—because nothing is happening, this ship doesn't move, at least not the right way, it doesn't sound right and now it doesn't move at all, stock-stiff in the whirl of waves, no ivy upon its oars, when should any ivy have grown there?, we don't have oars. They are superfluous. We've got the motor but that's a no-go. Who walks on water? I spare myself the answer.

The children get nothing to drink, they might as well get used to getting nothing to eat either, let them inhale the wholesome diesel smoke, that'll do, yes it is diesel, not a new word but, as if out of thin air, in everyone's mouth, hot breath that was to blow on the ankles, but it doesn't come, the ship can't breathe, it is still struggling for it, but nothing's coming, even though it's got the diesel, a modern fuel, which nonetheless has been around for a long time, you can even heat with it: but, it smells funny somehow when it gets burnt, when too much gets burnt up, when it doesn't get burnt all the way, that was not the plan, burning up that much, getting burnt that way, abused for fraud by the *Volk's* car, that's not how it works, cars being so cheap and not doing much, which isn't their doing. It doesn't work. This car does not drive quite right, the diesel is no good, the diesel is tainted, it drives only two power wheels, all of mankind has been put to the test as everyone trembles whether it will pass, will it fulfil its own specifications, how could this work with only two wheels? I ask you, what do we do with just two wheels, what do we do with the other two in the meantime?, we need at least two more for this vehicle, ideally each driven separately. Or another option, conversion to manual operation: then we'll still need at least one person to work on it. Unfortunately, none of those will replace a motor, it might run if it has to. But then the pollutant emission might be too much, who knows? If we adjust it to reduced pollutants and feed it enough then it will run poorly, it will splutter alright. However, if we adjust this person—who already exhausted himself looking for work—to optimal performance, he'll have to siphon less fuel for himself but he'll be able to race along, on the roads, on the assembly line, everything will glide, everything going down smooth, like honey, no jam as in traffic. It will create quite a stink and more dirt than before, it will pollute our environment, so then what are we going to do with it? No idea. What is the desired conduct? Depends. It depends whom you want to protect, yourself or your world around here, the forest, the meadow, the river, the lake. I don't read anything about people here. I know how much I can eat sustainably, that's enough for me. There is a lot I can't tolerate which the environment still could for quite some time.

The sky is leaden but at least it isn't falling, that's all we'd need, we are on our way down ourselves. Wherever we are, it's going deeper and deeper. The board of directors steps up its damage control, luckily it's not stepping on us. So let's say, the supervisory board is in session but the cars don't want to go by the board, be supervised; they want the air we breathe to become foul and sinewy like cats so it can carry us, the air-filled boat. For that, however, we lack the supervision for all these people here. They do what they don't want to that's all they can do. The boat is crammed up to the rim with them even when they are lying down there is nothing to get a grip on, polluting the air won't help the motor if it still won't start!, it could do that also when it's working, please motor, poison us but run, just start running!, away from us isn't possible, so just run for the hell of it like the city marathon runners, they are also running, come hell or high water, who else would do that voluntarily?, only the one who must. Nothing but water around here, the motor has a defect, that much is obvious. Those Volkswagens are not defective, they are just too cheap for what they must be able to do and they are too expensive for what they cannot do but should be able to. I want to buy such a diesel car please, I'd take out the engine, pour in the diesel and put the engine into this boat with the spluttering motor. So that it finally can move on, it's about to give up, the motor, you'll see, it'll give up completely in a moment and be done with. it. And what will we do then? Honesty does not cause us any damage, a busted motor does, especially when we must move on. On this oar ivy is slowly growing after all, but we don't even have this oar, we assured you several times that's no reason to insure us for what would we do with an oar. But we are in a hurry, we are in a hurry for nothing. We can't live forever without breathing. Hello, can someone lift the fog, can someone give us a lift, any plastic container would do, there are so many drifting about here, the fog bothers us. Though we see as little without it. But that's not fog, that's just breath, you are welcome to use it, if you don't need anything else. Oh, you also need your hair wax, which you always carry with you in your backpack, so that you always look pretty and fashionable when you have to present yourself anywhere. I understand. The desire for beauty, I can understand that. The child inhales the diesel exhaust gases, it feels nauseous, can we please put it some place else? No we can't or we'll upset the balance, besides we have to take care of the wrecked motor. But if it's wrecked anyway there's nothing to take care of! There is nothing we can do. We have the swim vests alright but we'll drown nonetheless, no idea how but we'll manage. And if we don't, we will be rescued, we'll arrive and throw out the vests at the beach as if they had not been little lifesavers, which kept us afloat for a while, we won't need them anymore, those airy wraps which could have saved us if it had come to that, if that fishing trawler had not come and taken us in tow. We cannot know that yet, someone would have to first make a call and reach someone.

We throw everything out but ourselves. The throwing out is over now, now comes the taking, crouched at the fence, wrapped in the barbed NATO wire, just move a few moments, for a test only, between Hungary and Slovenia, you'll see how that hurts!, and you'll take it down again right away, that didn't work, the ingenious Ulysses wouldn't have messed with it to begin with, he'd have invented something else. Now life is approaching us again, we had given up already, now suddenly arms are embracing us, our hearts burst at the sight. Is this life at all?, we still can't see very well, at long last, welcome!, the sea is deep blue but now at least signs of aliveness are increasing—mud, junk, trash—as if we had anything to throw out, a cast net?, no our innermost product, that's what we are throwing out like weapons, their shells, crouched down, always crouched down in the deepest shadow of fences and gates. Compared to that the sea was still deep and blue, but we do welcome the shallowness and the beach beyond it, with still more junk, that's what people love to produce the most, not cars, no, junk, also comes partly from the cars, it's all very confusing.

We teeter like ants under the carcass bits of beasts they are lugging, but we aren't falling yet. That's good. The motor is dead. We aren't yet. There is a sun lying on the water, can someone rescue it please? It might be drowning too! No it won't. The motor is down too, it won't come back no matter what we do. It can't be revived. The morning sun overtakes the shadows, but that does nothing for us, there's nothing in it for us! We swim into the light like that dolphin-man, the motor didn't work properly then either, not as the man had told us, he promised that the motor will hold up for a while. It's not-functioning might actually be the way it functions, like your so-called functional clothing or something like it, something that functions, but only when tested in storms and water, so that your parka, your functional pants will prove themselves when put to the test, you'll see! But I doubt it, all we knew about this boat was where it was to be cast off. Now it is time to tell our names, only no one wants to hear them. What city will thrive all around us tomorrow? None whatsoever? Only water? Say, by what name were you called back home? Maybe it'll be the last word you'll say. Everybody is called something as soon as his mother gives birth to him. That's right. That's how it should be. And tell me the name of your land, your people, your city too, so that our ships—with all thoughts directed there—will not take you there again. Because they are supposed to get you to another place. The Phaeacians' ships don't need a pilot—well, maybe theirs—but ours do, not even because of the rudder, reportedly, they don't have that either; you know in advance where our people need to be steered to; one look at us is all you need. And now we must steer ourselves but without a motor we can't do it and and with a motor we wouldn't know how. There are ships, we don't know them, those ships, however, do know their mates' intentions without being told and all ports of call and all the rich green fields, with wings of the wind they cross the sea's huge gulfs shrouded in mist and cloud. Okay, fine. But unfortunately we can't do that. At least the sea is still silent. Still! No idea, what ideas it'll get once it notices that on this ship we were steered into danger so as to never arrive. An escort would really be nice now, we could talk to the guys, we could yell something to them, they could throw us a rope, not a bad idea in this darkly swelling sea, we surely could use one. Dragging an enormous, protective mountain range around the city wouldn't be bad either. Well yeah, but not here. Here we can only dream about mountains.

The swell now smooth and shiny because it's not a swell. The dolphin-man who explained the motor to us, though not while it was running because it never ran properly, that man is now swimming back to the shore, he is already properly dressed for it. We are yet to reach the shore, the other shore where we want to get to, I don't know if we can make it there, there are lawns and pretty creeks, which we don't have back home. But surely we shall see big hotels and well-lit restaurants. And good people who'll bring us something, a pizza maybe, a bottle of water, a piece of bread with something on it. And say something to us. It means nothing to me but there are some who understand them. There we can finally let lose the vehemence of our desire. If only the motor would run better! Do something about it! The man in the green swim trunks steps ashore and pulls out the money he made with and from us. And when we will have disappeared, there'll be no more evidence, once we drift pale below the algae, there are none here?, say we, the jellyfish. The swimmer's arms turned into branches, wish I could swim like him! He'll celebrate with his milk-brothers tonight, hey, he did it again!, once again he made a kill collecting from people the breath of life, it was their entrance fee into the sea. They all paid, otherwise they wouldn't have made it into the boat. The sea will collect on top of it. First the cash, but the sea must be paid as well, we'll have to think of something, we still owe it the rent, we've spent almost everything already, fifty dollars to sit on a chair, three-hundred-fifty dollars for sleeping three hours in a bed, it says so here on a slip of paper, it has been checked so it is true, I only just read it, supposedly it is correct but what good is such a check! Can't say that about the motor, can't say it overspent itself, and one certainly can't say it had been checked even though we paid for it in advance, that was also one of our expenses, we, however, are so many. How much is the ride per meter? Specification and reality diverge, but we won't notice, because it wasn't us who had to tank up. Now it's filled with diesel, the motor, it's about to puke, and that was also an expense, the fuel, a considerable one, and that doesn't yet include your food, does it?, and no, it does not overspend itself, it doesn't even give what it has. It gives nothing. The Volkswagen at least gave what it was given, it owes nothing to anyone. Not even a zappy way of driving will get you more, for then you'd have to constantly refill that little tank with that conveniently clear emission-cleaning fluid! A small wonder, this car can't even do a thousand kilometers with it the way you ruthlessly race this capable road raft as if Diana with her dogs were after you to turn you into a stag. She's got a lot of work to look forward to. What are you saying? Those who created it, this condrivance, were also capable of something? That's probably true, still, they were in no way incapacitated, there is no evidence whatsoever. Then the surprise at the gas station where we suddenly owed something they had promised us before! It was to be a saving. Some kind of clean world, and this particular vehicle would produce it with this clear liquid, it will contribute also to your life, unfolding bright and clear, oh yes, indeed you can be absolutely sure of it. All you have to do now is pay. But that's not too bad, you can fill her up yourself, no problem, check the manual where the tank is, one and a half liter will get you up to thirty thousand kilometers, that thing about one thousand really was too pessimistic, so why all that fuss? That's how far the purity will get you, which you can pour into your tank like a few last prayers into your soul, that's also how far the purity takes you with a catalytic converter, that's the other option for purification, in that case however you'll you have to get the converter clean again with the diesel-fuel injection, but that'll also work albeit not by itself. Everything works but nothing works by itself except yourself. Everything always works, just not for everyone. And the best thing about it: you can do it yourself, no need to get all worked up! You can personally pour it in, all you need is a funnel, a canister or a fuel nozzle and everything will be clean and pure again. Or there will be a clean-up. And while we are at it: who says we are to blame? And who are you to put the blame on us?

This boat won't give or say anything, it spits for a while, long enough to get off the shore and not having to look at sand or rocks anymore, and then it is silent. People were so happy it did anything at all, the motor, but it didn't do it right because now it's completely silent. It only started with difficulty and it must not stop at all or you'll never get it going again and then you'll have to keep going yourself, but whereto?, as long as it's running, it stays warm just like a human. As long as it can run it maintains the proper internal temperature to survive, it could not warm up but it had enough residual heat to run, hundred, two hundred kilometers, this one can manage, but the other one over there doesn't, nothing can be done about it, but the one I put my money on can do it. Just that it should also be able to swim, but that's too much to ask from any motor, they all run out of steam in water. And consider this: because of the rocking of the boat, which is not its own doing, dirt must have been washed up into the tank which cannot be removed, that's like those madmen back home who are granted status by the people, on borrowed time that is, and thus must be returned again. A loan is a loan. Wealth could do a better job but that's not been borrowed. You better remember that because I am not going to say it again. More often than not you can get old wrecks like me into gear only if you get them warmed up somehow, like that marine engine, so now I am just running hot until you put a stop to me. You can hold a lamp up to me, well maybe not an open light, but a shaded lamp, because I cannot hold on to me, I can't do that, yes this is how you have to hold the lamp!, so that I can warm up a bit and then get going. You don't want to? But I would like that.

One can no longer hear the motor, no wonder it's no longer doing anything. It had been running just long enough as a promise to get these people to the island of Kos or any of its neighbors, now it can keep this promise just like carmakers who give in to any pressure, first the air's which also would like to breathe, then to the customer who is able to breathe on his own, then to the sea, then to the emissions calculator. Oh no, that can't be right! And those people also gave in to the pressure and bought swim vests and small water bottles and energy bars, but you won't get energy from them, we already consumed the energy and then barred the gates behind us, that is to say all the energy when we still thought it was cheaper.

When I think of the drama they made of Hector's corpse! And that was just one man and nine days of outrage from the gods. But our motor not running doesn't concern them at all, it doesn't concern anyone but us. Because of one man who is now a corpse they have been arguing for nine days now, and because of thousands of men, women, children they don't create nearly such a riot, oh well, those will rot all on their own. I have to look up how that works in water where they will bloat, men, women and children who are also corpses as of now, and soon we'll join them, thirty or so more and another thirty or so and still thirty more, more or less right over there a few more and surely today many more boats will arrive! Those are the lucky ones, they won't become the deceased here, not yet anyway, that was the prophesy and the gods collided, screaming, but luckily those people didn't get between them, yes, exactly, lucky them, the gods didn't fight about those for a change. The gods are fighting over this Volkswagen's lie, and that one's too, a car from which one should be able to demand high standards cannot be that cheap. Our expectations of this boat were much more modest, it was the minimum requirement, it should run, it shouldn't run out, but it does not run. So there it guzzled diesel until it almost puked, it rattled a few times and now it won't run for the life of it. Who'd want to quit running? But if it must be, if it is the water's wish, if it wants to fetch us in our youth's greening year to follow Ulysses's trail in the water. Something isn't working. I think fate decided perdition. In case it has decided something else I'll find out in this magazine, which is our mirror, our *Spiegel* which always brings in the big guns, and I will sing how the cities were destroyed by the refugees until the real guns will be hauled out, there won't be any other way. And the wind, what does it say to that? The wind won't work—can one say it like that? Does it let its back get savagely beaten by its enemies, the various vehicles? That won't be necessary. The wind won't blow, no matter what, no matter what pitiful lot you threaten it with, if it will not blow. It doesn't move us along either. The wind doesn't start. The motor doesn't start. It is as if everything conspired against us. Perhaps, a small sacrifice? Sacrifice, anyone? We don't want to become victims but maybe that girl over there who is making such a pretty drawing right now? You want to sacrifice that girl? Come on now, that's ridiculous! That's not a sacrifice! We make that kind of sacrifice every hour, in case it is required. So how do we go about the sacrifice, we have to start somehow and somewhere. What star travels its steep course right there? Why does it climb up to the zenith, while we must go down? Not a sound all around, well now, are we getting on with the sacrifice or what? The wind, that idiot wind is silent, it wants screams, so it can pass them on and that's why it is silent now, so it can hear something when it starts. We are stuck here with twenty-seven people and a dead motor, do you understand? We must have a victim, any volunteers? That girl, well, that's not a lot, maybe the gentleman over there?, the lady with the headscarf?, no? So this girl must suffer, I mean, suffice as pledge for our crossing? Well, I don't know but in any event we won't let ourselves be crossed. So then Victim, over here, would you like a stone? What for, a stone? For you to lay down on? Whoever is not assured of divine help will plummet into the abyss. And the crowd? It's shimmering, never satisfied senses cause nothing but chaos. And you are a human whether you like it or not.

Well, if our children have to lie in their own shit and breathe sick diesel smoke from a sick motor, then we have no room for you girl, there, lie down!, we'll tell you where to lay and off we go, don't stall. I am running, I am running, where on earth do you want to run, you can't even stand here, can't even lie down for the sacrifice, and yet there must be a sacrifice. Don't let slumber beguile you, you sacrificial victim you, you wouldn't be one if you were to experience this unconsciously, that's not how it works. No wind, we wouldn't have any sails for it anyway, no motor, but you are here, our sacrifice, you were called and now you will be killed. No rolling by on speedy wheels, my child, to the ships of the Greeks, there one is coming already but we are not Greeks, but that's who we want to get to, and that's not a ship, that's a car that's also rolling along, only it has too much power, it burns up too much for that power and that doesn't even include that effective fluid; yes, exactly, the one for cleaning, the cleansing fluid which must be clean itself, no, you can't use water, even though it's as clear as it is invisible. It won't happen to us, that we, like the capitalists, will be allowed to love change and to settle here among you for a change. We are driven out everywhere, we drift away, it happens all by itself, it happens on this ship, it's the only one we have. Before we go, dinner in the orange grove, that's listed in the program, we insist on it!, dolphins dancing around the prow, I declare, the party is over now. Favorable winds to Naxos, Kythera or one of the neighbors, what are their names? Donkey boys, dust, deserts, Jerusalem, baksheesh and an endless fuss over passports. We haven't got that far and we won't get that far because we don't have passports. First we must journey to the faraway ocean, oh here we are already! On our boat trip think of us, you—our sacrifice, think of home, think what you want, maiden sacrifice. What are you saying? Mother is coming along, isn't she? So you are seeing your mother there? No. So she doesn't seem to be there. No father, no mother, you all alone, off to other people into a foreign house, but first the sacrifice, that will save you all your troubles while we will invest our savings in taxi rides, to Germany for instance, and if we can't pay, the taxi driver will cut half a pound of flesh out of us, but we only go to the border, we must also walk across alone, all alone, all of us alone, all of us.

Not so fast, we are not there yet, we still have quite a ways to go. And we don't yet even know which way. So far there's no way for us to even be on our way. We'll just have to ride the surf on those boards, then a quick selfie before it's too late, because the boat doesn't want to go on, it bucks, it needs to get rebooted, well, it had to come to that. We'd be happy to just get one meter further with the same diesel, that is the same amount your Volkswagen inhales per minute. Five million cars are affected, we aren't. No one cries for us. Just a moment, something pallid fell into the moon shaft, let's do a count if it was one of us! Only one? Do colors clash in your blood because you aren't affected? We however are destined for consumption by the ocean and we are against it. No matter what the ocean wants, we don't want it. Sure, shyness and love belong into the heart, who does glory belong to? I am told to the Peleid and his Pallas, the Germans' goddess, fine with me, but what's left for us? What's left for us humans to do? In his heart's madness the former held Hector beside the curved-beaked ships and did not redeem him; beaked?, weren't they curved and also resplendent?, whatever. All I know is: our boat is not beaked. It is packed with people, chock-full of mortals, simply too full, but resplendent it is not. What? With gifts we should please, no tease, no, appease the gods? Anything else? What's left for us to give? Ourselves probably, that's what the gods always want, well, okay, then we'll give ourselves to them if the girl we chose is not enough, we said that all along. Unfortunately, one of the gods has already left, he had to be home for dinner, that's what he promised his divine wife. The one who has power over us because the boat belongs to him, yes, also the motor, he already jumped ship, no not the motor, that—how shall I put it—that man who made promises it's not his fault, the boat isn't his, the money is, we could have bought many boats with it, one for each of us, who wants to do the math, please?, on the other hand: the boat is made for sinking, if sinking it must be, then rather there, where people are swimming naked in rivers, snuggling up to more beautiful ships, which don't need coastguards because they are in a marina. There, now he swims like a dolphin, the owner of this boat, but he also bought it used, from a third party, it'll be sunk anyway or sink all on its own, why spend money and for a motor that works we could find a better use, we better put it to use where we can get more out of it for a longer time. Now he jumps high up in the air, that man, straight from the water, I can clearly see his tight green swim trunks, I seem to be obsessed by such trunks, always have been, well, by what's in it, it warms my blood tank which does not have to be refilled, I am self-cleaning, I don't need to booze to run smooth. Now the man who got us the boat is swimming ashore, away from us, as quickly as possible, far away from us so he wouldn't get into the maelstrom created by us. But we also want to quickly get away from here, though in the opposite direction without approaching traffic, because everybody wants to go there, we drive on water as if it were land, we drive, wrath is duty, but no one around to receive it, no god to throw dice for us, not even for our robe, no society that would exchange us, we wouldn't know for what. We are worth nothing, we could be given away, sure, but no one would exchange us for anything. We are doing everything we are told to do, everyone except those cars on their wrong track, all doing exactly what they are told except it was the wrong thing. Those motors were promised long lives, they understood, their life was competition to which they were challenged mockingly because they were too cheap, they are ready now just like their buddies, okay, and now all the buggies, no, bugs and boats will be taken back, taken home. We however depend on their help to get away, obviously, without wrath nobody's body, possession and liberty are safe, so lets get this wrath here, it won't do us any good either but we'll take it along to be on the safe side, it's in this waterproof plastic bag, not the Peleid's one, together with the phone with the pictures of family, house, land, diploma, all gone, all gone, but the pictures want to stay a little longer, not for long, just for a short time, our wrath lies right next to it, that's where we put it, because inside us it's of no use right now, it will stretch and purr, it will jump up with a snarl, I am amazed it didn't do so sooner but there is too little room here for sure. Lynxes and leopards, sure, they jump. Not us, so—are we sheep, as it seems we have no rage? It must be somewhere, we took it off somewhere, we did, and at least the boat isn't yet sinking, it does everything it shouldn't, but it does not sink yet. So the motor is in place but useless, so what about our wrath, where did it go? We haven't yet told whom to direct it against! If you want wrath, you'll get it! I want to see the day when slaves—no I'll say it another way, I'll say something else—the day when wrath won't be necessary anymore. Here it is, I found it, it was next to the last jar of baby food, here's the wrath, but even that won't get the motor going. I don't understand. The energy is in these bars, locked in behind bars and this wrath is—not the Peleid's, not this time either, sorry—nothing again, our wrath is in these baggies. It must have everything in its proper order even if this car uses up more energy than it took in. That diesel rides in this car here, in the one over there a swig of diesel also goes down smoothly, only our diesel here in the boat stays put and does nothing. Maybe it would do something on concrete. Maybe we would do something else had we enough to eat.

The man in the swim trunks explained the motor to them, that must do, he is already stepping ashore, he swam across and now he steps ashore, he steps up to the beach, to his friends. If deeds are not bundled and stock-piled in the heart, exhaustion will follow. Should I be indebted to that man in a swimsuit? Well, not I, that's for sure. So I don't owe him. He must own up. But who cares. And the sea couldn't care less. The motor has had it and the people have to have it, something to eat, that's not possible, go some place else. The motor did eat, it ate the diesel, which didn't do our darling Volksbuggie any good because it lied about the amount, it wanted more and it got it too. But we should have been told! Yes, you, but not everyone. As punishment the motor will be torn out of it alive, ouch, with its two golden eyes it had covered the land and cut through the air and sawed through the woods and it lied all along. It can no longer do it, period; it cannot run as cheaply as it claims, it ran afoul of its own specifications. Wrong. Its brain, the soft ware must decide what it wants, it's always only one or the other. More foul air or more fuel in the tank, one or the other. Minimal fuel consumption for good performance, so why not go hog wild, beautiful nature right and left, she'll hold up a while longer, yes and the lungs too, no worries! And what's with that body there, under the water, it can no longer accomplish its task, we are really sorry. Alright then—it's either carefree racing along dry roads or, other alternative: less pollutant emission, it'll just have to guzzle more, that speedster, there's no other way. Well, he's got problems! Everything that costs is a problem. I would know what I would choose. I would definitely choose carefree. And that wouldn't only do for the test station, it would always work, for normal operation we simply switch the consumption of Spic and Span and Mr. Clean, of Pronto and Besto or AdBlue to almost zero, and whoop-de-doo off we go, makes our hair fly backwards, you won't know what hit you, it's a great feeling for the car too of course, it won't have to worry about anything anymore.

Unfortunately this boat can't do any of this, it can't choose, this boat can't pick its own motor, and if it does, it can't do much, and it doesn't have to do it for long; it's operator designated this motor for the boat and now it's supposed to make it work, not much, really, that's not necessary. And if it croaks we don't have to pay for a funeral, it gets a burial at sea. The manual for this motor and that one too—for everything that has a permit for the sea and won't stay calm if water seeps in—states, keep going all the way to the other shore. But when the motor has had it, the whole thing doesn't work. Between mountains that aren't here, between the water that's aplenty all around, and through clouded blackness, the poor boat works itself into the ground. It can't go on. The people, who must keep going, can't do it either, but at least they don't need any fuel, they are fuelled by something I don't know and that's what we will hang on to now. We'll hang together and will be saved while the brothers are still torn apart.

And we forget how to return, we forget how to get ahead, our eyes see what had been told to us back home but now we are looking at something completely different. There used to be a military power before us, behind us, everywhere, it stood in front of our soul. Now we fear every cat of the wood and the lynxes on our hats, no, no, the German armored *Luchse* looking out for us, leopards eating grapes, vines growing in our worship. Come on now! Stop it! Okay. Considering that something can be said any time, I might as well stop now. Oh evil bird hovering over my speech. Do you still want to say something now? I must die, so many standing around here and I have to die, what, you too? How so? And does anyone dare to bear down on you? Everyone! All of them! All!

Only a few splinters, no more, out of:
Ezra Pound, Cantos
Euripides, Iphigenia in Aulis
Homer, Odyssey
Thanks also to Philip Hagmann and the Deutsches Theater Göttingen and to Wikipedia *with its many cars!*

APPENDIX

The conquest of the world as image, that's history, for an image is made to stay. People however, are not made and they don't stay where they were made to stay. They fight for their position, that's not a position as you might imagine, that's just staying the way they are. They gave up on setting a new standard for *being,* for the set has not yet been set up, the one they will walk into. But they walk. They keep walking. No suntanned cheeks but sore hearts, tear-trained, they weep, they know how to, they better do, they have to, all of them except doctors and seers who are already drained of tears. What, you had three children and now there are only two, the third, who also happens to be three years old, is suddenly missing? That's nothing compared to others who are no more, calm down! They are moving along. Those few men who once were so important to me, so dear, like kin on their terrified flight, many already gone, some accused, they took someone along on the train, the train did not complain but here they were stuck with a claim, I don't know, I forgot how it turned out, they probably are still around or maybe not, those men who remained, some even here with us, I don't know. Whoever drew the line, judge, savior or smuggler, there had to be a line, something's always on the line, for them, pulling them, this way, that way. And they also get in line, lining up, moving on. They do have a goal that crashes against the Hungarians' Christian arrogance, but our tribe still takes care of them. Internally raging greed but we are still fighting against it. I was overwhelmed, compassion overwhelmed me and also other things, for example, this morning I was overwhelmed again but what of it, what of it, I am sitting here in my little house, I get overwhelmed just by a single gust of wind knocking on my window but not coming in as soon as it sees me, or the drunk, probably someone from the neighborhood whom I don't let in, I shut the window, I shut the door, period.

They wander around, those people, there are so many, no one can overlook them, they are talked about, no one can understand them. They are, like, you know, they don't know how people talk here. No wonder no one bothers to listen to them, not to their suffering, not to their songs which are of no use to anyone but them, those songs one hears, to the guitar, to an orchestra, you get to hear in a show, where people present themselves, those who really are presentable and real, and even more than that: who produce sounds of sorrow they've drilled into themselves in front of a mirror like shards of glass one has stepped on, something's hurting and it must be looked at whether one likes it or not. Isn't it piercing, the rehearsed pain of the woman singing in this show?, she would gladly let it get inside, if it came in person, that obscure pain of desire. Life is so hard, she sings breathlessly, but she still has enough air, luckily they all got airs, what torment in those songs soaring from the device, the torrent sears through it, such torture, those songs, and the woman sings so beautifully, yes the man too, but that's not what I wanted to say, this program was going on with-out me and will come back three more times this year, I don't mind. How loudly they wail, those are real cries of suffering, yes go ahead, hold on to them!, those folks camping here—let's hope just temporarily until they go away again—are measured by how real they get their wailing across, such loud cries of woe, glaringly shrill, dark, dull sounds, tear-dewed. Those tones of woe are sung now by that other woman too, I did not see her yes-terday, tomorrow I'll see others, but today it's her turn, please, where is her third child, her three-year-old daugh-ter, where, I ask you, who can hear it, tell me, really hear it, please! No idea. It's easier on TV, and even more on social media, there you can choose your own visiting hours. In reality those are only bytes, bitter bytes, not in foreign sounds of language unknown to us, no the woman, the singer sings in German and they all now want to learn German as fast as possible, those camping out here, wrapped in blankets, scarfs, foils, oh no, they are so stiff, they can hardly be twisted around. The singer's wailing sounds are so loud, you have to tear open the window so that the sounds can get out again, or they'd shatter the panes.

Alright, anyone else shattered here? This mother, who lost the third child along the way gets comforted, pro-vided for, something gets written down to help find the child again. Or she'll just be gone and that's that. Then it will be a funeral song. That's okay too. More than they deserve, the way they sit there picking shoes from the pile nobody sorted. Are those the right songs, the right tears?, is this the right kind of suffering? I wouldn't be surprised. They hope that something, ideally everything, will still turn out to be their hell, I mean *Heil,* and Germany has not yet started to shoot, at least not in the sense of buds, well, okay, but of butts, it constantly kicks butts while the Bud keeps flowing and everyone stays put, Germany is there to stay and it is at the helm, it fights the salty waters, which isn't hard, their sea is way up north, but that's where they want to reach too, those besieging are beseeching us now. They want to get to Germany or Sweden. In Sweden they can complete their studies and after five years become citizens of that land. Who asks, who wants to know what happened before, in the ship's house, to others, to no one, to many, what happened that even without a storm a gentle breeze brought them here and still they capsized, whose fault was it, it was their own. They never complain about it, they have to put up with it and now they are here alright. They produce volcanoes of shit and dirt and waste, it looks as if a mountain of waste had exploded, go ahead take a look at the mess they make and something like this is to live among us now, and for good? They don't pass the German course, because they don't get in, so they make it to us without a pass, and did not pass the course that all of us would pass, because we can flee unscathed to wherever we want, so instead of learning their lesson they produce a lot of trash, for good advice comes at a price, waste is free, since WCs have not yet been invented in Hungary, maybe invented but didn't yet make it all the way there, I just heard that Serbia has exactly the same problem, only worse, so I should not talk about Hungary, but I will anyway. The fence is closed now. A train came and closed it with NATO wire, now I should say something about *NAHTOD*—near-death experience, that is—it would fit well, they often really are near death—if they haven't already died at sea—even though near enough, so that they would get to have experiences, and if they did they wouldn't say.

Calculations always contain violence. Ulysses, for example, one of the most famous travellers had calculated his journey to and back from Hisarlik Hill in Turkey but was delayed by so many events, yet he had a return ticket—I've no idea how long it was valid, and how often it had been punched. The world must find an indispensible form, otherwise nothing will move, but how many lack any form on the paths they follow, on the tracks they move on from sleeper to sleeper, not to here, not to there, not this time, they obediently follow the tracks that determine their route, but this is also why the trains can't run anymore because the people did not take their seats but occupied them instead. Those tracks have been occupied. Someone always gets the bum rap because he is the last one. Only yesterday Mercedes was in the factories of those Germaniacs and sorted their human stock into useful and useless kinds, that's quick and easy for them, or they wouldn't have been so successful, sure thing, their god is not a remote god, God knows, that one there isn't even a god, who on earth believes in that one? We wouldn't be so successful if we believed in him, says the Lord of Daimler and takes down the names of the men who know how to do things, who arrived as suppliants, each waving a branch, soon they'll hold screwdrivers or whatever, which that robust messenger, that union buster, the robot, man's priceless helper, that's pricier than any human and enjoys replacing him, does not want to put in their hands because then he would be replaced by humans!, and we, once again we are getting the waste left behind by Mercedes, the used Skoda or the refrigerated truck that changed owners a few times and now doesn't have one at all, at least he doesn't come forward, our star points somewhere else, and it's not a lucky star, speed unknown; no, nonsense, known, we all know how fast this car can drive when it wants to! But people can't catch up that fast, they don't catch on so quickly, they press on, but—no, not to get to the battle of worldviews, they might win that one. But not security. They cannot win that prize. Not against us, because we can't include them into our lives or conclude that they are us or relate to them as ours and our lives as theirs.

We already have relationships, we don't need anymore. We would like to relate to this breathless singer not the naturalized one, that one does not have to be naturalized, she already is, she has a right, she is just right when she sings and dances and laughs and wails. Unfortunately, a good view is no longer an option for me, there are too many viewpoints now. One has to first review what there is to view, this program: yes from the bottom of my heart, yes! The way she sings she must have settled here long ago, because evil peoples don't have such songs and they don't want them either. I am not watching her, that singer and her super show in which she comes flying through the air, what a lucky duck! I could—no, not fly—watch her, I have a device for that. If I'd ever want to hang myself, I wouldn't want to be strangled in that singer's slings but there's no danger of that. The danger comes from others, thank God, they got away, and where to? To us. So there. A better view can still be worked out, no, another view won't work, I already have one, I'll be happy to hand it in, in case you need one. I already have one view, I don't need a second view, I already viewed my fill, the second one would be too much even for me, even though I secretly have several for different looks, those I have up my sleeve, let's see what happens, in an emergency, I'll pull one out and hit someone over the head with a knock-out argument. The next one better not be my brother or it'll be a real hit, I'll smash his head in. It cannot be my brother and he can see that too. You can see, it's just awful what I have to look forward to, and every day a different look, I've got my back-up views well in advance, in case one, the older, outdated one, needs to be updated or cleaned. Now I am looking through my eyes of the day, I see my views of today and I present the following to you—yesterday all of them were still human. Today I cannot look at them since yesterday thousands, tens of thousands more arrived, and already the charge of injustice has arisen. We make spot check-like controls, which, however, are not very controlled. It is pure willfulness, but it's useless anyway. I have quite a different view of control, right, mommie dearest? How can thousands be controlled, how's that supposed to work, those spot checks do not hit the spot though we have the best removers, I can't bear the sight anymore, I can't stand it but at least I haven't been befallen—by grudges, by anything, I've sprung from a new mold, I offer you something new, don't you see, be happy, here you get only the newest, otherwise you'd have to get it from the papers or the TV or the hystery book, the only place where you won't find me, my nerves wouldn't be able to take it, but the radio will tell you too, I always say what others are saying, I wait until something new presents itself to me and then I throw everything into the same empty bottomless pit where you also throw anything you have no use for. And already I resort to my latest view, shouldn't I better take the other one, the one from yesterday? I don't know, there simply are too many, and too many people remain who were not here before, that's not possible. That many are not possible for us. Where could they go to, where did they come from? That's how they imagined it, but that's not the way it goes. Just getting here was troublesome enough, because they lie so much, they are not the ones who they are, but their getting *to* and getting *in* is a no go for now, for we go by the book, our hystery book, from now on there will be controls. The getting here will be stopped and thereby also the getting ahead. Maybe this baby, this child can get out, one got lost already, a three-year-old, I am curious whether she will be found, and many others didn't get away at all, not even by the skin of their teeth. We will have to change our knowledge about people, but the knowledge resists. Whatever it knows it wants to keep to itself. It will never be as it was before again, just the fact that it knows of these people, of these objects will make a difference; con-sciousness, I am afraid, will have to change its knowledge, there won't be another way, and that knowledge alone will also change the object itself, it will change us all, please listen to me, as long as I still speak, as long as I am the one I am, as long as I find these objects, these people as objects, my knowledge still pertinent, not pertinent—rather pertaining to my knowledge, which is very small and least of all I would find them appealing, I wouldn't even know in what language—so, as long as I find them, the people, not language, I have it with me, I always have it with me, here it is, hello, my language can handle it, it'll manage alright. Nonsense, I know where to find them, the people, the objects of my thinking, no, can't call that thinking, as long as I find them as presented to me, how do I find that?, much reduced and in this device and exactly at 9 am, 1 pm, 5 pm, and then three more times in the evening, and when I find them, these fleeing folks, none of them will stay on, because they are so fleeting, then nothing will hold on and I won't be able to hold on to myself, I can't even now, as you can see. But I won't find anything for me to hold on to either. Neither will I find my own standard for that. That's what happens when one embarks on a journey, so and so many of them don't make it all the way, the rest make it to here or they die because they wanted the rest of the family to get here, too and were it only away from here. Then why do they come here first, if all they want is to get out?

Transportation? Discontinued. But now what?, what's up now, now it will be resumed, but also controlled, tomorrow controls will be reinstalled and transportation stalled again. For now the train has been taken out of service, in an hour it might resume service again, I don't know. Who would want to be of service to those people? Good folks with food and clothes they can do without, want that, let me express my special thanks to you and I have many special expressions for that but I'll save myself the trouble, for which you'll soon thank me, maybe already tomorrow! Inscribe my words in your hearts if you don't have any paper at hand or any other device that records them and stores them, at least my words should have a place to stay. No not those, we want other words, from others. Who, I ask you, should record them? There aren't enough devices anywhere to record them, even though their stories are interesting, and even more so, if they are made up. Oh God, now that crowd gets moved towards me! What should I do? Turn off the device before it overheats? But it will get lukewarm at best, like me. There are so many, so many people, who have found their destination at their earlier stops, but, not anymore. Now, we are their destination. Those are humongous crowds, they require planning and guidance and being led—on and off—, if they cannot be kept here any longer, like in Hungary. They are a needy lot who are a lot of work, many won't do the work, and then they shit in front of our house and dump their waste right there. Where should they take it, seeing as how they haven't yet invented the john in Hungary, much less in Serbia; I mean the portable john, one of the most important inventions of mankind, who wants growth, construction, production, reproduction, where are construction workers to go, but those are a manageable lot, they also manage to see the john right away—always in eyeshot, so that too much valuable construction stock(s), meaning construction time, is not lost, right?, that little blue loo we all know hasn't yet made it to Hungary. I think it was intentional. Ulysses, come here, take a leak, I mean, look, no, I mean: listen! The song of those creatures can be somewhat distracting, if one wants to be distracted, we could use those singing females now, not the sirens, those are all yellow, dressed in sequins and they get pulled upwards through the air as they sing, they are singing in the skies, like that woman who sings very loudly and amplifies it too, so that absolutely everyone can hear it, well, basically we need such women, we'd need many more women, but none would be like that breathless woman, who can breathe much easier than us nonetheless; women who sing that way and divert the gaping crowd, that would be the way, maybe we should fill the packed station platforms, those are very dangerous, with her smoky sound, no, you can't smoke here, that's a no-no here, and it is in force. Let her go elsewhere—who?—well, that one there, though it does not have to be exactly that one, but she should know how to sing. Yes, it would help if singing women could manage to go some other place where they have johns since we do not make any available to you because as soon as we get overwhelmed with such giga-planning, we'll stop planning altogether, right, huh? And in Serbia nobody plans anything, who'd want to go there? Right. So then we'll just discontinue planning.

That gigantic mass of people, they make 'giant-like' a quality of its own, I think, this actually makes a mockery of the quality of those people for having none. This mass moves here, because it was told to, then there, because it was told something else, then it stops again, nothing doing here, nothing to be done here and there, where they had arrived, nothing either, and the children play with stones at the soldiers' feet. Those stones have been there for an eternity, like the name of the Lord, it stays forever and ever, it stays with us. Those fleeing have another Lord, they take him with them when they leave. The altar, even during times of war, provides protection to all fugitives in dolorous distress wherever gods are feared. Yes, so? The Hungarians have no such fear, and now they no longer let them pass through either, and soon they'll have a fence, a brand new one, which they are building right now. Those people must go elsewhere and there are many other countries people are assigned to, but not all of them accept those foreigners, those lost ones, at least those they found, holding their smartphones as unreliable shields, which often tell them something wrong, just as we do. Those are people just like us. Those are phones just like the ones we have. No, this country is not Australia. Germany is over there, across the green border, which you, however, will not find, for it is green no more. They don't care, I mean, those countries don't care what skills those people have. Who needs them? Okay, they might have qualities, which could possibly be brought to bear, but Mercedes has already grabbed those, and their quota already maxed out. We don't need more people now. We already have enough. We have enough of them already. I always say that at this point. If you are interested in me, you know this, this is the truth of my mind, which is very small.

The void gets stretched until it screams and then it finally gets filled. And still it isn't content. Let me help stretch this emptiness, so that more people can fit in, but it's not possible. This void is already full. Everything is full. Everything is brimful, so many, so many, they might be amazing in their way, well, okay, in their ways maybe, but now they are just emaciated, so first let's get them something to eat, yes, thank you, they can have that and also something to drink and a roll mat or a sleeping bag. They do get what they need, if not right away. Patience please! If that's all you need. Because we need to move on. No, we don't have beds at the moment, they have those in the Swedish camp, unreachable, but we still have bits of floor in stock. Floor is on sale today, patience now, there'll still be plenty left tomorrow. Not only is every humangous mass of people different in size from other humongous quantities, it also invents its own definition of size. This one here is simply too big for me, not only for me, don't you have a smaller one? Even Hungary might have portable toilets for a smaller one. If only it were smaller, that mass, if only they were fewer, these people, they could at least enjoy their excretions, those can compensate for a lot. They could compensate for father and mother, for there is much to learn from the sexual activities of children. The lips suck food, if there is any, as to other zones, pleasure must be compensated by muscular activities. And this creates the following problem:

where to put it, if one isn't a child, but just plain small, an insignificant member in a humongous crowd, there isn't much that member can do with it either. Genital excitability could be the lifelong consequence if excretion can't find its place—wish I had your problems!—and in case of a child, it does not want that place, it wants to take advantage of this excitability of the anal zone. I am telling you, in case you have no children, I don't have any either, but I read about what's going on with them. Yes, the child likes doing that, maybe that three-year-old, the one missing, does it too, let's hope it has been found already, even though it's a little girl, she counts for something and has genital urges. It wants to hold back those pressing masses, the child, you can read up on this, you won't know more than I do, holding it back, so it can enjoy the strong sensation on the mucus membranes, that's a nice activity for our little ones and smallest ones, but what do the grown-ups do, if they don't have a place and the function of discharge is prevented, after they had already been deprived, freed of everything they had, house, apartment, business, family, relatives, friends, what do our grown-ups do in Hungary? They have taken this route, they were right, right so far but not anymore, as of today. Tomorrow I might no longer able to tell who is right, then a new pass will be trampled down, a trail marked by the sign of the supplicants, which they will travel along harmlessly, but nonetheless in some state of agitation. A new trail, coming from the messenger in their device, according to the messenger's word, as to what's where, how should they know?, informed by the electronically winged messenger's word in their hands, they are now travelling along this path that gets them where, just a moment, I have to check, it must be Croatia or Slovenia or both, but not today.

It has only started today, their going elsewhere. But today is no longer yesterday and yesterday the following was true: what a way to start!, I mean, things started yesterday, hold it, not so fast, I can't keep up with myself, but those people must think on their feet, still, their device is faster, it must be, for who else should tell them what road to take, which path to stay off, lest they'd be beaten and now it's already a wide road with white swathed—the supplicants'—signs, Refugees Welcome!, but first another look at the display which tells them something, it tells another story because Hungary doesn't want them, Hungary itself is a gut that wants to purge itself of those unclaimed people. Who's supposed to stomach that? I ask you. Like it or not, it doesn't work. This country says: Get it all out. Even the Church is powerless against that. Get it all out. That's not what a child tells its gut because it wants to keep it all in as long as possible, its shit is its first gift, it has nothing else, the child, it is a gift whose refusal expresses the child's defiance of its environment. But who wants the defiance of all those adults? There is no destination for them, there is only the road they trampled down themselves, after they were trampled on by the Hungarian photographer, oh no, that was just one or two people plus their respective children, they have experienced worse. It doesn't even have to be broken, that anger, there is no more need for it, that's why it gets nipped in the butt. It doesn't have a destination, what destination could it be?, even though those defiant ones have lost everything, where should they direct what they can't keep inside forever? It has to come out at some point, it can't be helped; what would help: the porta-potty. Welcome, little blue friends, there you are, nicely lined up, people never line up so orderly as those guys do, what else can they do, they have to line up to get into those little cabins. For the least little bit they have to get in line, and that's nothing! They should be happy it's not worse. Here you won't find one portable Dixi potty, an entire Dixi band, a cohort of those blue Dixies would not be enough to take in those crowds without sword or cross to shield them, that is, who don't have the guts to fight the real shit—anyway—no Dixies here to take them all in for even just a moment, no, take them out in just one moment.

How then should he express himself, that angry man in need to press on, if all he's got is right inside him? No one is interested in what he's got in him, it's too much already that he is in here at all. He can't even let go of his shit after he held it inside for so long? And that woman with the red spot on her pants? She is ashamed! The child knows no shame, but that woman is ashamed. She sits on the side of the road and is bleeding. Only a grown woman could come up with such a thing! And what got into that one over there, a thunderstorm's brewing and it also erupts, and off we go, hurry up, the bus is waiting already, and of course the woman doesn't want to miss the bus, she has been waiting for it forever, attention, breaking news! That one's in labor, can you believe it, really!, only grown women could get into that. Okay. She's taken to the hospital, let's see what I can find out about her condition, at least in the hospital nothing will happen to her. And I've been sitting here for such a long time, I sit and sit, though I know how unhealthy this is for grown women, sitting, ask anyone. I'll die of it, sitting here, but not yet, that can take quite long, thank you, she is doing alright at the moment, the woman, yes I am too. Let's take a look what the crowd is doing, what these people here in the crowd are doing. They board the bus minus one woman who is in the hospital now, having become two persons, get two for one. Those folks must make do with what they get, or they just head out on their own, when the train doesn't come or is an hour late, they don't want to wait that long. They head out, there is nothing brazen in their voice they know they must control themselves or the Hungarians will lock them up too. They don't want to lose their place, in fact they haven't had one in a long time.

No way to get over that fence, but if that one's already too high for you, you haven't seen the fences in Bulgaria or Greece!, nevertheless!, please use the regular crossing and, most importantly, do not use the irregular toilet, which calls itself nature but in the meantime has turned into a far cry from nature. And now? What will we do now, if we are not children, get no children and have no place for what we have honestly acquired with the food, if we got any, which we now want to birth through the bowels, to bring into the world, it's not as bad as a birth, but it still must come out, and this end product, which is what becomes of donated meals no one is in charge of, there is nothing and no one, it is a loose end, what's man to do if he can't tie ends together, he would have to connect his mouth to his ass, in a sort of short circuit. Oh well, money, shit and the word. If we could spare ourselves these three it would be okay, but unfortunately we have nothing to spare and nothing to save. They do have mobile phones, the supplicants, but the body also wants to decide and defecate, oh no!, those two American students are already holding Kleenex to their nose against the stench. Let's be honest, that stench really is unbearable. Special masks are already available, policemen wear them in Hungary, I don't think those protect against infections, they use it against the stench. Here you see, there you smell an activity that doesn't know its destination, well, yes it does, but—where to? It would be better if those folks knew their goal even better, they really should, where will the stench go, where is everything supposed to go, including that which isn't even there?

We do know where to put the telephones, first to the charging unit, then to the ear and then back again. But where to put the bodies that come with telephones? Nobody can be imagined without a body, but by their phones you will recognize them. If the escape is to be free of bloodguilt, a smartphone is needed at the very least, which tells you when, whereto and how. Their shit, on the other hand, they would like to get rid off, the flight-ridden, because without such letting-go everything's a no-go, without letting-go everybody would burst. What am I saying? No one wants these people, that's the long and

the short of it, there is no place, there is no place for anything or anybody. Excuse me, just now a hall has been
opened here, military tents over there, and there we
opened the waiting room for bicycles for them, let the
bikes wait some place else, many, no, not many bikes
which had taken their spot, their place, many have the
runs already. Where to put it, a bit here, a bit there? How
those people bop around with their poop is revolting. We
can do that much better, but we don't do it. We bop and
bounce elsewhere, we run to wherever a marathon takes
place. There are so many camping here, they'd have so
much to give but don't even have a little room where it
could all flow into, where they could be at rest while it
happens. I have my own notion of size but here it falls
short, it doesn't cover this kind of mass. I also have my
own notion of beauty, which you can read in my face,
still!, it won't hold up much longer just as Hungary can't
hold so many people or would want to, so much vanity
showing on my forehead, right there, where the eyebrows
are, I do smear quite a bit around there when I adorn my
face with color, no peace in my eyes, my gaze restlessly
flitting about, am I beautiful enough to go outside, even
if it's just to the supermarket. I like being indolent, I am
not hesitant. While I write I can do anything and I take
advantage of it, who could do me any harm?

But you, I do not recommend this to you, who are on
the run, for you are foreign and fleeing your country, the
weaker ones better remove their big mouths before they
let it rattle on, I'll remove my make-up only afterwards,
after the people will have seen me. But I am all by myself

so I can easily do something others are not permitted to. If you beg for pity from a stranger, you shouldn't be too loud, but not too soft either, lest you won't be heard or left unanswered. You should simply be, you should just *be*, that's all, take it or leave it. What else can one do? There'd be a lot left behind but it should not be ablated, it should rather be sublated. Or better still: leave it to Hegel.

The crowd is gigantic, it has grown humongous, but it must not be growing here, it must not take roots here; and all the planning, calculating, I mean all the facilities they need, starting with eating, sleeping, education, defecation, all those installations for security, they go way beyond my notion of *calcul,* I am not good at math, but this wrecks my brain, and what must be calculated becomes incalculable. And what needs to be said becomes unspeakable, well, I can't say it, I should be able to but I can't. This mass of people is surrounded by an invisible shadow, another mass hidden away, an uncouth, ungainly shadow that's cast wherever food is thrown at them, where their feed flies through the air, hey, there it flies, a drone?, no, what is it?, that's a roll, you want it or not? Someone else will love to have it if you don't want it. This decision is taken off your shoulders, someone else has caught it, he was faster, we are sorry. If you don't want the next one I'll take it, yes and the water bottle too, it's even more useful; if you don't watch out, it'll crash on your head! Your shit's running down on you, don't you notice?, where, I ask you, should it go?, where do you want to put it now? They are always in such a hurry, thus man becomes subject and the world an image, but the hurry is not the reason for it and what's to become of this subject I don't know either, it should join the line maybe it will get its turn for something, no idea. I don't know, I don't know, I can no longer oversee it, no not even over-look it, I can't, I just can't. But I don't have to either. Its not my call, I can recall it and then watch TV or browse along, I don't have to do anything, I have to sit here end-lessly, in front of my device, forever, which as I said isn't good at all for me and my body. And it wouldn't be for you either. If you know nothing, shut up, shut your mouth already, I hear, I can't really see it, the direction it's coming from; we have it coming from so many sides. If you can't see through it, keep looking at the screen, yes the big one or the small one, whatever you've got, there the world gets shot from a fox hole, big or small whichever you've got on just now, so now you've seen it, there is no more and now you're on your own with the picture, serves you right if you can't grasp it, not even if it's small. What you can't grasp, we grab. A fence, after all, is also a grab bag. And it will now be locked up before a few million Hungarians are up for grabs because they are under such massive threat.

This gigantic space, this gigantic mass has long gone way beyond my imagination, and even the unpredictable has disappeared, someone else has already computed it, there's no way out but those people are still on their way, even if every clock were to stop, they'd still be going, they are moving ahead, but that's got to stop!, are the borders open, are they closed, are the trains running, are they not, is the highway open, is it not, are there check points, are there none, are there checks now or in five minutes?, randomly or thoroughly?, all unpredictable, all more than I could know but no more than what I could find out on the radio, on TV, on the small social market in my hand, that's always open, that's more than I could find out but did not have to pass on because you saw and heard exactly the same without being able to figure it out. You now must go to the Department of Revenue, where you'll be told whether things will end up well or badly for you, whether the eyes of finance, not of high finance of course, can look at you full of grace or if you will have to pay more than some others who haven't paid anything yet. Come on in hurry up! Already by noon everything could be different, that's what makes it so hard for fiction, there's hardly time for a photo!, it's running out everywhere, the shit is running out everywhere, in Hungary where they don't yet have porta-potties, where you can't get them anywhere, yes, yes you can, I have seen them in some places, not in person, naturally, out there in nature it's all different again. The trains are running again but there are controls, because of them you got stranded in Salzburg and you got impatient, so you walked to the town of Freilassing, it's name suggests it sets you free and it surely will live up to it and not lock you up, last stop, end of the line, no, not last stop, still moving on. Nonetheless, it's a good idea to have something ready that proves who one is, it would be best the world would rise beyond its present space towards a new determinacy, which I definitely won't be told about, but I don't want to go on a trip, especially now, that the trains are so full, a determinacy, which won't be determined for me, let alone for thousands, don't read the old odes, my son, but the train schedules, they are more accurate, but more accurate than what? They are not told anything and I am only told what I could hear just now—most recently a quarter of an hour ago, the next one I won't wait for anymore, on the radio and on TV and won't see on my tablet which has nothing on it or everything when it's turned on, they don't say anything to them, they do tell me, but it does nothing for me, it is too much, it's too much for me. It would be best, if I can make a suggestion, they could rise beyond their predestined, designated space, those people, then they would finally have room, which they would have made for themselves, they do not wish to be seated close to God, for they'd be dead then. Then all this would finally be finished, their determinacy would become something unique, which, however, will not be visible. Could it be seen, everyone would immediately clear the way for them, but there are too many, no one stands alone and no one stands out as unique, there simply are too many moving along here, and there as well and over there more than ever.

Those who were in the church back then, who requested sanctuary, they are nothing now, they weren't even a beginning. Now all the world's the stage and it expands into a space not predetermined as theirs, so that everyone can come in, so that their shadows can also come in, so that their dead can also come in, who've also become shadows, rushing over the living, they can't be considerate, they have to take care of their own determinacy, which we determine for them but they have to find out nonetheless, and then we have to tell them their destination, which does not coincide with the one they had in mind! Mind you, there is nothing we can do about that. You have to find it on Google Maps which your relatives sent you, who are already in Sweden, they do know their location, the GPS does it for them and from that location one can let oneself be sent via various routes, you can enter anything, what would you like, what means of transportation do you want to take, and this is what you want to get computed for your destination, so you always enter the latest positions, the device always knows where you are except if it is an outdated device, so then you have to enter it, then you must tell it, your mother in Syria doesn't know, but the device knows exactly where you are, and then those in Sweden, who are already in the best location will choose the best route, the fastest route, no traffic jams, no weekend traffic, the best routes are searched by those who are already in the best place and in safety. So it goes back and forth because you are moving back and forth. Everything gets determined elsewhere. So it ends. And then it continues again. Maybe you'll have to wait. You and all the others who are walking with you.

Not even your shadows point to where you should go, the shadows are made for you by the sun, but where you are is told to you by hand-painted town signs, no, they use templates for that, and then they enter the names of the towns for Sweden, and then the route kicks in on your device all the way from Sweden, showing you the way to get away from those who want to kick you out, sorry, that was cheap, but true. Cheap but true. Even you can afford it. Those masses of people won't even find out what has been denied to them. What's been denied, I've said it already, are those potty-cabins. They really did it to me!, they don't do me any harm, they don't do anything to anybody, you might wonder why I am so obsessed with toilets, because I sit on one so frequently, that's why, and the Hungarians deny them to people who would like to have control over their excretions, but they always miss the mark. The toilets are never where the people are to begin with and that is also where it ends. The way in is up front, and in the rear the people are coming out again and it's coming out of them, now please, where should it go? Now look, this place here is as good as over there. This escape, do you think it it's true that it happened out of a mix of humbleness and arrogance? Is this the reason why everything is denied to you? Is it here right now, the moment in history that belongs to you and that god, the Sun god, who is also a refugee from heaven, he knows such bitter destinies, but does not want to share them, he wants to drive alone in his fast vehicle, it is a two-seater, but he drives by himself, he is driving across the heavens, he knows his destiny and the human lot, those lots of humans, yes, that's why a lot of others want to get rid of them, people, when they become too many and it becomes too much for us.

And the ground where they are staying, that's the only one they got? Did I, by spreading garbage all around, garbage everywhere, crap, shoes, parkas, caps of the dead whom I conjure though I shouldn't, could I have ruined the ground?, but wasn't it already ruined before? By spreading the rotten, the misbegotten and exposing the dead and forgotten, you can easily call attention to yourself, you are somebody, after all you shot and uploaded this picture and now it is working for you. Make up your mind if you want to publish it, if not, it won't matter either, it has no consequences unlike this text which might be followed by a sequel. No. No worries! Zero consequences. Just this one I think, nothing will come to my mind. Too many people are coming here, I can't wrap my mind around them, I gladly welcome them to our land but what else can I do? I never even share my house, not even with friends. I don't share, I just let you have it. Haven't I said that somewhere already? With absolute certainty. But that only comes with death, he'll soon be coming to me, I am certain. Just you wait, you won't hear much more from me and then you'll have to respond yourself, not my way but yours. Take a look and say something about it, say what you are going to do, what are you doing tonight? Avoid hostile blood relatives? That's no problem. You simply say you don't have time today, period. But those people won't listen. Not your relatives. I mean those foreigners. Those people flooded the lands, they are here, they are there, they are foreign and they are in-between—no the in-between is the screen, that's where I watch them, on-screen and I scream—in print, watching out for oneself is better than meeting friends. The screen comes in-between, we need better screening, but screening won't help. There is no time. The child is dead. The other one has just been born. There is no time for lingering on the cold shore. The picture has been taken, it will be shown to the world, period. Only one, a little boy. Big deal.

No answer. Just now something is brought in again, no idea what. The current inflow will have to be stemmed, no, the Danube won't stop flowing, well okay, you can channel her, on the left and the right, it must be done or she would be the ocean, but you can't stop her course, she just keeps flowing along, no doubt about that. The soul, oh yes, it can swing wherever it wants to, we swing ourselves over this fence even though it was meant to be insurmountable, we use every hole, we can also crawl, we throw a blanket over it so it won't tear into us, the fence, no the fence won't tear, it'll rather slash us, who knows how long they'll still be there, those natural loopholes. And today they are already gone, and fourteen people have already been arrested and will be locked up, soon there'll be more. What does Europe say? Europe says nothing. What's there to say, we founded it but sadly we have no longer control over this construct, someone has to execute judgement unto these crimes, but no one does. The God of the Dead? Is there one? And if so, which one? Anubis, the jackal that eats dead matter? Well everyone knows that one. Take one that isn't that well known: Thoth? Controls the weight of hearts and writes down the results? What are you saying? He is the judge of crimes, I can't think of his name, oh right, Thoth, I just said it, and who is he?, but who judges the living? Supposedly, he does that too. And anyway, how am I to talk to you, says this or that helpless god, it doesn't matter. That hole in the fence might pop up some other place, no that's another one, who knows how long that one will last. We have to get through them. The operation. The processing. The jurisdiction, but not for the conditions, we mean the location, which more often than not does not even fall under Germany's jurisdiction. The national specifications, the national explications, the national abominations. There are so many, they'll just have to accept that they don't have the choice as to where they want to seek shelter, because our helpfulness must not be overextended, no, no that's true because it is written right here otherwise I wouldn't know it. Something should be imported again, which we've already exported, border controls, so that not everything we don't need can be imported, which Mercedes doesn't need either, that star who classifies people into usable and unusable. Points of departure, of origin, need to be established, but those don't even know themselves, where they are coming from. The border control will find out, everything must be accounted for. No mortal eye has ever seen so many fake Syrians in one place. It doesn't matter anyway, that woman here is lying for sure, yes, and that man over there is too, they all lie. They speak the wrong language. There are too many, we can't control them anymore. The place of refuge must be moved, it is no longer here, look for one yourself. That's what you thought, wasn't it, didn't you, when you set out on a ship, maybe because it wasn't a ship, not even a boat, just a dinghy made of inflatable rubber, one prick and it is gone. The smuggler jumps out in his swim trunks, no not out of them, he swims away and gone he is. It's not that bloodguilt drove you into banishment, oh yes, it was bloodguilt, whatever, what are you saying, oh, it wasn't yours?, doesn't matter either!, and we also carry a lot more bloody guilt, a heavy debt that cannot be paid off. By the city folk's decisive resolution something must be done, I won't bother writing down what that is, for in an hour those city folk's masters will have resolved something else again. Which woman rejects which man, who lost his child, who's losing his right now, who is having one right now, during a severe thunderstorm no less, the word severe goes with storm as the word heavy does with punishment. It's all one. Sometimes there are more. To me they have seemed more than all for quite a while. Like spectral appearances, they can't be compared either to anything else that appears. The people flee, they have been fleeced, that means they have no funds at all, doesn't matter, they'll get more gifts of fleece en route, no not the golden one, that came ashore in Greece, not to the shore where the dead are lying now, that is if they ever made it to there. I don't know. Yesterday it was Germany and Sweden, I don't know what it is today.

This city here, that country there, the graves they've been dwelling in so long, the crap they throw out, that corner where they shit, that foot on the ground. What ground? Was that yours? I'm sorry, then I will look for another ground for my fast rowing vehicle, let me through, I am its auxiliary motor, something must help them!, no, the ground is for myself, I no longer have a vehicle, though it certainly brought me here, but now I have to manage on my own. I was sent by the sea, and that was lucky. The tornado, thunder and lightning, the rain-heavy hurricane, the howling wrath with which we faced the salty waves only to be able to finally face you here, you whom we never wanted to face, all over, twenty- three, no, I just hear twenty-seven of us are dead, they dropped, they drowned, thus deceased, they ceased to count, we however, we seize every bed we can get, for the ocean certainly won't leave his for our sake. There are no dry diapers for the ocean. And we are now boarding this train despite your refusal, but you will get us out again, we can see it coming, right after we cross the border, if ever we will get that far. Our God shall be our Savior, but you don't like that one either, you don't like anything, we can see that already. So we call out the name of our God, we've brought the mobile phone, we call him, on your flowery ground where nothing will grow again, after we will have risen again, we are thinking of our forefathers, we are thinking about our foremothers. We step before the inhabitants of this land but we want to get to Germany or Sweden. That's probably not believable, or rather that is what we really want, but we don't believe we'll ever get there, we just hope. Whatever is believable, if anything at all, will be revealed tomorrow, when we'll know the new regulations and time will have torn up what's been said, then we will find out too. Then the sounds of our mobile phones will roar into our ears and we'll be able to understand the call, we interpret the flight of maps on the displays, always a new one, it depends, thus they fly past as the falcon chases the nightingale. Driven from our country's groves, our river's banks, we grovel for a new home, no wonder you can't hear it anymore. Today you still can but tomorrow it will be getting too much even for you. And we, we are beat as well. So you don't have to do it anymore, the beating. That's at least something we can relieve you of. Anything that goes beyond our immediate being here, we can relieve you of, because soon you will no longer be able to do it. The progression of our destinies is unstoppable, oh if only we could be there already, where our destinations are! By then, our destinations will have progressed further than us, you'll see, so will we, unfortunately. The destination will be where we won't have to go beyond our limits, where it will find itself and the notion of Germany corresponds to the destination Germany and the notion of Sweden to the destination Sweden. Our progression thereto is unstoppable, you can control as much as you like, it will always be limited to our natural life, you cannot control more than that. If we get torn away to death, you no longer have a say. You are too dense for that, yes and there's already another one of your dense fences. We'll climb over it or crawl through from below, and on we go beyond the barrier, it's behind us already, and the void ends or a new one begins. We shall see.

The usual as before. With a pinch of Freud. Well, that's all we needed!

EPILOGUE

My Coffees with Elfriede

Elfriede Jelinek leads an increasingly secluded life ever since she received the 2004 Nobel Prize in Literature, and no longer gives interviews in person. As her authorized translator I have had the opportunity of many visits and inspiring conversations at her homes in Vienna and Munich. In this context she agreed to the extensive conversation reproduced here for the first time. The informal tone reflects the nature of our relationship as collaborators and friends.

We met on three consecutive afternoons in the modest two-story house in Vienna-Hütteldorf on the outskirts of the Austrian capital. It is her family home where she continues to live after the death of her mother. It is important to note that Jelinek does not see any productions of her work due to an acute anxiety disorder and thus depends solely on reports from her friends. Spring and summer 2014 turned out to be an especially active period. Six weeks after *Charges* opened the quadrennial Theatre of the World Festival in Mannheim, Jelinek's *Faust/In and Out*, opened in Munich as part of the Residenz Theatre's Spring season. The repertoire was devoted to contemporary explorations of and responses to Goethe's *Faust* (on which he worked throughout his professional life). The program included lavishly provocative productions of *Faust, Part I* and *Part II*, as well as variations on their themes by new playwrights. Jelinek's text is one of her so-called secondary plays. It is an addendum to Goethe's *Urfaust*, his early version of *Faust, Part I*. In her characteristic dramaturgy, topical concerns and canonical texts, motifs of Goethe's youthful tragedy of underage Margaret, seduced by the middle-aged scholar (based on the legends surrounding the medieval story of Dr. Faustus) and driven to infanticide and madness, provide the basis for her take on the monstrous case of Josef Fritzl that shocked the world when it came to light in 2008. Fritzl had lured his eighteen-year-old daughter into the basement of the family home, where he kept her locked up for twenty-four years and fathered seven children with her, one of which he allegedly burned when it died a few days after birth.

At the time of my visit Jelinek was greatly relieved that she had just finished her most recent and longest performance text: the 230 typescript pages of *The Silent Maiden* (*Das schweigende Mädchen*). Johan Simon, the artistic director of Munich's Kammerspiele, had already begun rehearsals for the play's premiere scheduled for the following fall 2015. The play is based on the long-running trial of Beate Zschäpe, in Munich. Zschäpe was one of the young leaders of a Neo Nazi cell called the National Socialist Underground (NSU), that had begun to organize in the eastern states of Germany after the fall of the Berlin wall and continues to attract skinheads and other disillusioned youth across the country. Suspected NSU members were routinely recruited as spies by the German equivalent of the FBI and local government agencies. During the trial it was revealed that government agents were aware of murders and assaults planned by rabidly racist skinheads groups in both eastern and western parts of Germany, but did not intervene. Pertinent files in these matters were quickly destroyed. The title of Jelinek's play refers to the defendant Beate Zschäpe, who so far has not said a word during the entire trial. For twelve years she and two friends, who had also been her lovers, Uwe Mundlos and Uwe Boehnhardt were on a murderous rampage against people with a migration background, killing at least ten, possibly more. After the police was closing in, the two young men were found shot dead in their charred camper. Police investigators reported that the gun in Mundlos's hand indicated a murder–suicide.

At the time of our conversations the trial was still proceeding without an end in sight. As a consequence the text of *The Silent Maiden* was very much on Jelinek's mind, while I was still deeply affected by the Munich opening of *Faust/In and Out*, which I had attended the evening before our first meeting. Consequently, references to both works kept slipping into our conversation which was, however, primarily focused on the text of *Charges*.

GITTA HONEGGER. In your performance texts, you inter-
weave topical events with canonical texts, from the
Greek to the Bible to Nietzsche, Freud and Heidegger,
to name just a few. How do you find and construct
your themes and their cultural framework?

ELFRIEDE JELINEK. It was clear in the case of *Charges*. It
had to be *then* and it will annoy me for the rest of my
life that it couldn't happen right away. Because it was
planned to be performed right then and there. I wrote
it for a special occasion, for Nicolas's (Stemann's) project *Commune of Truth. Reality Machine* (*Kommune der
Wahrheit. Wirklichkeitsmaschine*) for the Vienna Festival in May 2013. I did not ask what he wanted to do
with my text and it simply didn't fit in. The project
was supposed to be an immediate response to current
events and Nicolas only worked with original soundtracks and direct quotes, news and such things, and
mine was a literary text and that didn't work. Looking
back, I think it still should have been done then with
two or three actors, just setting up somewhere,
Nicolas would have certainly participated in the
reading, and I would have probably read as well and
that's how it should have happened. And then it was
done in a church in Hamburg, which was already a

half-religious act in a way, it was very beautiful, apparently and it had a ceremonial quality, but now it no longer has that subversion and topicality. Now it's just a play.

GH. But when I am reading it now—and translating it, I read it very intensively. It is absolutely urgent and topical.

EJ. Yes, now it just happened again, those unaccompanied children, five-year-old children, who travel alone by freight train to the US, since there is no specific law concerning children traveling alone, they can't be deported and there are graves all along the way. There are special DNA teams now, they take the DNA of the children—that would already be another play, the DNA plants—and create DNA data banks, so that when parents search for their missing children, they can be located. And just today, in the Mediterranean they pulled thirty dead people out of the water. They were all in one boat; all of them were dead. And that happens every day. Thousands, thousands, so the play is almost too polished, too beautiful—one can't really grasp such things, as I can't really grasp this NSU [National Socialist Union] terror and only now, after I finished writing the text am I reading a standard book about it, which presents a chronological breakdown of it all since the re-unification and I would not have been able to finish the play *The Silent Maiden* (*Das Schweigende Mädchen*) had I known it all before. Because realities are so extreme, complicated and complex I could not have captured them with my approach, which is always standardizing [*typisierend*], lumping together and does not explore an individual but, rather, shows a general political perspective. I could never have written it otherwise, I'd be totally meshugge.

GH. How do you respond when directors or producers approach you with an idea?

EJ. For *Charges*, Nicolas did not come to me with an idea, he just said, do you want to write something for the *Commune of Truth* and since I already was pretty certain that I wanted to write something about the refugees in Votiv Church and their move to the monastery, I thought, that works out well, what I want to write about is happening right now, that'll fit and I didn't ask him. What he really wanted was of course not anything literary, not a play, he probably thought I would put some newspaper clippings together. I don't really know what he had in mind.

GH. As you were contemplating to write about the refugees' predicament, before Nicolas contacted you, did you already think of the myth of Io, that her story can be merged with the refugees'?

EJ. But that happened independently of what he did with his *Commune of Truth*. I took his project simply as an inducement to write what I had in mind. Because I thought, that it was absolutely topical, so it would fit into Nicolas's project. But it did not.

GH. If Nicolas had not talked you into—

EJ. I would have waited longer. I would have taken more time. And then I did write it at an insane speed, two or three weeks. Some things require that kind of speed and the haste of the language. The text itself has a breathlessness [that suggests both the writing process and the situation of the "real" refugees]. Then there are ideas for texts, which were triggered by others. Usually I don't accept assignments. Usually I write what I want to write. Sometimes somebody says don't you want to write a play for us again, there is and that, could you imagine writing about it and then I say no. Now *Winterreise* [Winter Journey], I don't know where that came from. Ideas were often triggered by the Munich Kammerspiele, where *Winterreise* also premiered. But now I can't really imagine it could have come from there. Because I have been dealing with Schubert's *Winterreise* almost my entire life, accompanying the most different singers on the piano, sometimes I sang it myself, I practically know it by heart. *Rechnitz* was interesting, because the Kammerspiele and Jossi Wieler, the director, wanted something on Luis Bunuel's film *The Exterminating Angel*. I hadn't seen the film in ages, so I watched it again and it was clear to me what to do. David Litchfield's book about the Thyssen dynasty, *Art Macabre*, had been published, and before that I saw the documentary about the massacre at Rechnitz castle, *Totschweigen* [Wall of Silence].

GH. And there also are appropriations of Nietzsche's *Thus Spoke Zarathustra* and Euripides's *The Bacchae*. Were those then free associations?

EJ. Yes, they were. Sometimes, as in the case of *The Silent Maiden,* I consider quite specifically what additional material I could read, Agamben or different interpretations of the Bible. Those are now pure linguistic investigations of Aramaic, which I don't know (*laughs*). But it's so interesting, that Bible research has shifted completely to linguistic questions. There are all those disputed issues in the Old Testament; those are purely linguistic investigations. It's hardly a question of content anymore but, rather, miniscule shifts, whether the Angel was here or there and said this or that, or if angels really existed. I wouldn't have thought that in the end everything is a matter of language.

GH. It also is your primary focus. And the Bible, I noticed, is an increasingly prominent source in your performance texts.

EJ. Yes, it surprises me too. I mean, I am not religious at all, I absolutely don't believe in a God, but as bodies of speech those texts simply are—you can't kill them and I certainly don't want to kill them, because first of all, they are incredibly revolutionary, Jesus was a revolutionary, one can't just ignore that. Some of the disciples were too reactionary and too narrow-minded to understand that right away, or too cowardly, it was truly enormous, what Jesus spoke of, I do want to keep that for its revolutionary potential.

GH. And you don't really put religion down.

EJ. Well, let's say I preserve the greatness, for example of the "Sermon on the Mount," those are incredibly literary texts, nonetheless, greatness has to be cut, down, but without making it little. It remains, unlike

Brecht: "The Big will not stay big / the little won't stay little . . . "[1] I preserve the big and I take it down as the big. So it is a certain reverence, not the one of God or religion, but of the greatness of the texts.

GH. Did your mother raise you religiously or was Catholicism just an important aspect of Austrian culture?

EJ. I attended Catholic elementary school. Actually, I did grow up quite Catholic since earliest childhood. During vacations in Styria, there were our long walks from our house to the cathedral, the famous, huge Cistercian Minster, that's four kilometers one way and then back, even as a small child, I probably owe the last little bit of physical conditioning to [those walks]. Yes, Catholic traditions did have quite a formative impact on me. And of course, it is so much more mystical, as it is also in convent school, those quiet hallways with the nuns disappearing in their locked wing of the building. After all, I was only four years old when I entered convent school.

And my mother's mother, my grandmother tended toward religious mania. And my mother actually had visions—I sneaked that, partly hidden, into my plays—well, I think she really was crazy, angels really appeared to her and talked to her, so let's say,

---

1 Eric Bentley, 'The Song of the Moldau', *Eric Bentley: Songs of Hanns Eisler* (New York: Folkway Records, 1964). Available at: https://-goo.gl/zH9ENO (last accessed on November 28, 2015). Original German lyrics was wriiten by Bertolt Brecht with music by Hanns Eisler for Brecht's play *Schweik in the Second World War* (1943).

to some extent I grew up in a very mystical environment, which was counteracted by my scientific,
Jewish father who was completely atheistic. He and
his family did not believe in anything religious, they
tore Catholicism apart, in addition, he was a Socialist,
such a staunch socialist, like many Jews, that for the
workers parade on May 1, I had to have red ribbons
in my braids and then, on Corpus Christi Day my
braids had to be tied with white ribbons for the pro-
cession. In the US they probably don't know all those
traditions, Corpus Christi processions and such, in
Boston they probably do, and in Chicago with their
Irish and Polish population and the Italians—

GH. —and Mexicans, especially in the Southwest, where
I live.

EJ. Yes, of course! Mexicans have a completely different
Catholicism. They perceive death as marvelously col-
orful, while for us it is quite dark. Death. Even if you
believe in eternal life, in seeing your loved ones again
and on Judgment Day, when even our bodies will rise,
I don't know what'll happen to those who let themselves be cremated (*laughs*)—they'll rise as clouds of
ashes; repressed matter, the repressed ash clouds of
Auschwitz, they'll be coming on Judgment Day.

GH. The image of the ovens haunts your texts, I am
thinking of the production of *Faust/In and Out,* which
I just saw, about Josef Fritzl, who burned one of
the babies he fathered with his daughter. It was almost
unbearable to watch Johan Simons's minimalist
staging of the parallel monologues—the daughter's

haunting mediations on what happened and the father, the self-assured *pater familias* as her un-God. It was a theatrical experience that literally took everyone's breath away.

EJ. Really!

GH. It was that powerful. *Charges* is equally overwhelming, differently, because the text has such tragic immediacy.

EJ. Yes, that one happened in one throw. There are such things, they are written in one throw. They are just tossed there, very quickly, since it was written for this specific occasion, within two weeks or so, it is like a chorus, an oratory.

GH. Your text of *Faust/In and Out* features two speakers. The feminized Ghost and the feminized Faust, based on motifs of Goethe's *Urfaust*. *Charges* has no designated speakers. It raises the question, as in many of your more or less choral texts, who are the "we."

EJ. That depends. It has to be discovered who the speakers are at any given moment. That's probably what makes analyzing my text interesting, determining who those "we" are. Sometimes it is I who speaks in the *pluralis majestatis*, sometimes it's an ironical "we", it's something the masses appropriate, when everyone actually says "I," sometimes it is an abstract "I," so there are many "we's." There is "Bravo, we did it again!" (*Na, wir sind wieder einmal toll gewesen*) That's the collective, mocking I, that thinks it can do anything. And then there is the "I" that accuses, the I that indicts. Of course that's quite tricky in *Charges*, because everybody asks who is that "we," since I presume to speak as if in their voices in a way they'd never speak. But this "we" is probably the interesting thing in all my writing. Sometimes it is a role I am presumptuous enough to take on by turning myself into one of those refugees, something I am not at all entitled to, I live comfortably in prosperity and peace, I practically throw myself at them.

GH. Nicolas struggled with that during his preparatory work.

EJ. He was very concerned about me, a white woman speaking for people of color. I suggested he should read Frantz Fanon, the North African intellectual, communist and psychiatrist. But a black person can speak differently about blacks than a white one. And I suggested, that the whites should put on white make up and the blacks black, that is, they should make themselves up as themselves, so to speak, not the blacks as white and the whites as black, they should reinforce themselves. Moreover, strictly speaking, I am not talking about Africans. I refer to a specific incident, which involved mostly Afghani and Pakistani.[2]

2 The Hamburg Thalia Theatre prepared for the first production of *Charges* in the fall 2013, two years after Jelinek had written *Charges* in response to the specific situation in Vienna in 2011. In the meantime, the refugee crisis had escalated. By 2013, thousands of African migrants had tried to reach the Italian island of Lampedusa, many of them refugees from the civil war in Lybia. Hundreds of them drowned in shipwrecks in the treacherous waters surrounding the island. News about Lampedusa shook Europe almost on a daily basis. Hamburg had accepted about 300 of migrants from Lampedusa. The

GH. Interestingly, while I was working on *Rechnitz* and *The Merchant's Contracts*, it actually was postcolonial literary discourse that helped me understand your position as an activist, poststructuralist literary figure. The way you deconstruct and reconfigure the male canon, it's grammar, idioms and imagery, the dynamics of your relationship to the dominant language brings to mind Homi Bhabha's notion of certain writers as "comedians of culture."[3] The dominant culture sees itself reflected in the other, but still different, "distorted"—

EJ. Yes, and as a woman; in any case, as a woman one is colonized. One is doubly marginalized. On the one hand it is a burden one always has to carry: that a woman is not able to pull off a cultural creation, at least not one that counts, on the other hand it gives you—the woman—an anarchic freedom, of course, because it doesn't oblige you to anything, that's

public's reactions were comparable to the situation in Vienna. In fall 2013, eighty of those migrants lived in the Lutheran Church in the district of St. Pauli. The urgent situation inspired the *"Urlesung"* [*ur*-reading] of *Charges* at the church prior to the production. Resident migrants performed with actors from the Hamburg Thalia Theatre under the direction of the theatre's artistic director Joachim Lux. Stemann, who then directed the subsequent world premiere continued to include local refugees during the production's international tours. In one scene, the actors put on make on stage, each in a different shade of random color.

3 See Homi Bhabha, "Articulating the Archaic: Cultural Difference and Colonial Nonsense," *The Location of Culture* (Oxon: Routledge, 2004), pp. 175–98; here p. 195.

the point. And you are right with regard to the colonizing, especially in English, because everyone first learns English as a foreign language and there are so many pidgins and that is exactly what liberates the English language; well and American English is freer to begin with, British English is somewhat more fixed, but it too has this tradition of playing with language.

GH. And postcolonial writers confront the challenge, how do we speak this language now, the dominant language, can this be done without showing the rupture—

EJ. Yes, *discourse de maitrise*, the master's discourse, as the poststructuralists call it, language itself gets subverted by breaking it open or remaking languages for oneself.

GH. And this is what makes you especially provocative as a woman.

EJ. Yes, because it's not simply a matter of gendering, as is happening right now in this ridiculous debate about the Austrian national anthem [whether the line about being "the land of sons" should be changed to "the land of daughters and sons"], that's really dumb. The point is to subversively transform language, not just the use of "his/her" and things like that.

GH. It's also important to remember what you mentioned in one of our recent conversations, that you want to put your figures, or rather language itself on cothurns.

EJ. I enlarge my figures.

GH. Isn't this also due to your musical background? Those are not psychologically developed characters, but a composition of voices.

EJ. They are linguistic agitators [*Sprachkörper*] like agitators, *Rührkörper*[4] [literal translation, "language-bodies"; also "mechanical agitators"] which turn people into language [*die Versprachlichung von Personen*]. Basically, my characters are linguistic templates [*Sprachschablonen*]; that's of course exactly what I get criticized for—everything I say gets used against me. Everything I say about myself is used against me. It's like the Miranda warning.

GH. What makes it difficult for the uninitiated reader to follow your dramaturgy—at least while reading it—is to see the change in perspective, the "we" of the refugees and that of the local people.

EJ. Call and response as in Catholic antiphony.

GH. That brings us back to the astonishing religious resonances in your texts. There is a moment in *Charges*

---

4 One of the wordplays that are not readily translatable. A crassly literal translation, "linguistic bodies like stirring bodies." Jelinek's email response to Honegger, with reference to an editor's query on the German term *Rührkörper* (March 20, 2016): "There are many different sorts . . . they are small things, little balls, which help in the process of liquefying something, eye drops for example [that's what rattles when you shake the bottle]. There are many forms, also in technology." [Such as agitators in treatment plants, which Jelinek did not have in mind, though she might enjoy the connotation, albeit in a different context.]

Nicolas brought out chillingly in his production. It is the line "Let the little children come to me." In your text the speakers represent the local community. I quote: "Let the children come to me, we swiftly revoke their being if they call for their mommy, we drown them and on top of each coffin we put a little teddy bear. Yes, we top it off with more! Five coffins, five teddies! That'll do. They probably did not have those before. They had no coffins to play with and no teddy bears . . . " Nicolas turned the whole passage into a song, with the eerie refrain "And on top of each coffin we put a little teddy bear." During the very sweet mellow song that was sung by the performers along with projections of rows of small coffins, with a teddy bear placed on each one.

EJ. Yes, the teddy bear has become a common thread through several texts, maybe because they sit in that chair with a gleeful grin (*points to the transparent swing chair in her living room. [See image on the facing page.]*) They also found a teddy in the charred camper of one of those NSU guys, it was half burned, the teddy, they blew up the camper, the two NSU killers. An artist painted the whole scene, she also painted the teddy with those burned legs. Yes, the Teddy seems to pursue me.

GH. The "Teddy" turned out to be a minor translation problem. Your first reference to it is the Austrian diminutive term for *Bär* / bear: "*Bärli*" specifically for stuffed toy bears.

IMAGE Teddy bears in Elfriede Jelinek's living room.
Photograph courtesy Martin Vukovits.

EJ. Yes, that would interest me—how did you translate
"*Bärli*," the French say only "*un ours*".

GH. What came to my mind as an equivalent to the feel
of "*Bärli*" was the sound of Pooh Bear. But Nicolas
clearly had teddies on the coffins, which I did not
know when I worked on the surtitles for the German

premiere. And the image was so chilling in perform-ance that I did not pay attention to the titles. After-wards I was torn, since I really love that "Pooh" sound.

EJ. It has to be a bit childlike—as I wrote in the play, in their real lives those children never had a toy and when they are lying in the coffins, they get a toy bear put on them. It is eerie.

And then here are these two NSU murderers who killed ten people, maybe even more, which haven't been linked to them and there is this teddy bear one of them probably had as a child and he took it with him, that's even eerier. There you have the teddies on the coffins completely depersonalized—they were not the children's, after all, they were just put on the coffins to indicate that children were inside them, which was obvious anyway from the smaller size of the coffins, but that two Nazi killers also took a *Bärli* with them, that's really eerie—and the role of bears in my dramatic work . . . (*laughs*)

GH. And in your life, you have them right here!

EJ. And those aren't the only stuffed animals I have. Downstairs I have 200 monkeys, they belong to a friend of mine, but they occupy everything here—every window, everything, filled with monkeys, the hammock, the chairs, everything.

GH. Well, for the publication of *Charges* I kept the teddy, since that is the common image of the toy.

God takes on several meanings in *Charges*. Frank Stronach, the real person behind the unnamed figure of the Austrian Canadian millionaire, entrepreneur of automobile spare parts, and recently maverick candidate for the Austrian parliament—represents a sort of God figure. That was a bit confusing for my editor.

EJ. Well, that's the "we" talking—that's this one God, the "we" also speak of their God and that there also is a Jesus in Islam, there he is just a prophet that's why I realized I can't say "Christ," I must say Jesus, the Christ has been cut in Islam, and that's become Jesus, the prophet, he is not a savior, he is not God, only a prophet. God is Allah. Mohammed is also a prophet. And there are also angels in Islam, that's what I was told, I don't know much about Islam, only that what [Christianity and Islam] have in common.

GH. We have been talking about Catholicism in your work. That gets us to Heidegger, who keeps returning in your texts, who still is quite important in Catholic discourse.

EJ. Well, he studied religion, he was in a Catholic seminary. But he didn't last there very long. I think it was boarding school rather than religion he couldn't take.

GH. He is one of the main inspirations for your language based cultural critiques. Since your play *Totenauberg* [*Death/Valley/Mountain*],[5] which features Heidegger

5 *Totenauberg* is a play based on Todtnauberg, a village in the Black Forest, where Heidegger lived. See also "Death/Valley/Mountain," *Drama Contemporary Germany* (Gitta Honegger trans. and Carl Weber ed.) (Baltimore, MD: Johns Hopkins University Press, 1996), pp. 217–63.

and Hannah Arendt, he haunts all your texts. I got to know him primarily through you.

EJ. Of course, I can't say either that I really know him. But I use him selectively, so to speak. In *Totenauberg* [Heidegger] is the "leading text", so to speak as is Goethe in *Faust/In and Out* and Aeschylus in *Charges*. Actually I started around the time of *Totenauberg*, because the German reunification has, of course Germanness [*das Deutsche*] as its subject, which I dealt with in my earlier play *wolken.heim* (cloud.[cuckoo]-home)[6]. There, I started with just using quotes, in *Totenauberg* it was Heidegger, the philosopher, the philosopher of *being* and Hannah Arendt, who basi-cally had already lost out, but who already said one shouldn't take existential philosophy too seriously, one should also be able to laugh about it, this gives you a special sovereignty over it. With Arendt it is the story of emigration and the outsiderness of Jews, who must always wander—

GH. From then on Heidegger haunts all your texts.

EJ. But most of the time I make an ass of him.

GH. And Paul Celan, he also wanders through your work.

EJ. Not recently. But when he did, his presence suggested itself: all those stateless people, who persist against this self-assured notion of homeland (*Heimat*). That is, the thinker of *being*, in *Totenauberg*, who walks with his backpack through the Black Forest and Paul Celan,

6 *Wolken.heim*, literally, "cloud.home." In German the saying "you live in the clouds" means "you are crazy."

the Jew, who desperately tries to get a word of regret out of Heidegger, an admission of his entanglement with the Nazis, but he never got it, no one ever got it. Heidegger, who was a proponent of pure thought, who, after all, was very precise, in his inaugural address for example, would not let himself be pinned down to such a thing. Now in his *Black Notebooks*, which I didn't see, there apparently are more concrete passages, which I probably wouldn't have used anyway. But there you have a philosopher who thinks he can lead the *Führer*, the leader, and that an Adolf Hitler and his gang were just waiting for a thinker, that's so grotesque, gushing about his beautiful hands and blue eyes—but *Ungeist* cannot be led by *Geist*.[7] Nevertheless, I still see that Heidegger is a great thinker, I mean, I am not one, who kicks him down, down from the Black Forest. (*Laughs.*) It's making an ass of him with a certain awe.

GH. Did you learn from his method, did it influence you?

EJ. Well, if it did, I made fun of it. But of course, that's easy. Countless school classes made an ass of Heidegger. That's not too difficult once you get going.

GH. What is it that fascinates you about him?

EJ. The thinking. Pure thinking though that's, of course, mathematics—the purest thinking, and because it is not accessible to me.

---

7 An untranslatable term in this context because the meaning of the German "Geist" is "mind and soul," and the prefix "un-" denotes its antonym.

GH. But through your musical training you do have a strong connection to mathematics.

EJ. Well, not really. Music is a mathematical system, but the mathematical part of composing was always very difficult for me. You have to count and calculate all the time, how long is this now, is this now a quarter note, even if you work without measure lines or with different measures, you always have to calculate, how does it add up, if it's twice as long, what does it have to be then, a sixteenth or a thirty-second. A professional composer has that down. Olga got it down.[8] She no longer needs to count, but she has a mathematical mind. She once told me she has a counting compulsion, she always has to count everything and she can only have a telephone number that consists of uneven numbers. So, I am obsessed with language and with the mutations one can derive from it. Olga with numbers.

I am too impatient for that, as I am also too impatient to cook. Composing, you never can write down your ideas directly. There is always a complicated process of transposition until you can put it all together. Painting is the most direct process. You can put everything that comes to your mind directly on the canvas—one to one, simultaneously, writing is

8 Olga Neuwirth, award-winning Austrian composer, collaborated with Jelinek for several projects, such as the libretti for *Bählamm's Fest* (*Baa-lamb's Holiday*, premiered in 1999) based on the play by the Surrealist artist and writer Leonora Carrington, and *Lost Highway* (2003) based on the film by David Lynch and Barry Gifford's novel of the same name.

almost as fast and I think I am writing out of impatience. I can type very quickly because of my playing the piano and the organ, I actually type at the speed of my thinking, that is, I think somewhat slowly and I type very fast, (*laughs*) so it works out, I can put down what I think in real time, so to speak. But then it is many times. I mean, I don't leave it at that, but I don't tinker with it, I do it all over, again and again, and always very fast. That is, like someone who draws a sketch and then, by shading the things from the outside peels them out, so to speak.

GH. Whereas Peter Handke, your fellow Austrian—I think the two of you are such perfect opposites—

EJ. Handke writes everything by hand, in beautiful handwriting and he actually draws little sketches, while I write nothing by hand—

GH. He says somewhere that sometimes if he succeeds writing one sentence that's just the right one, it is a good day.

EJ. Hmm—but the pieces he writes, the way he writes them by hand, actually look as if they'd flow, you don't notice any hesitation or any starting anew, it all flows so smoothly. Perhaps they are already copies, I don't know. But he writes everything by hand, which I really admire, because I couldn't do that.

GH. You two—

EJ. Yes, we are antipodes.

GH. I find the comparison between the two of you, because of your completely opposite but equally indefatigable forging of a language, the German language, more specifically the Austrian German language after the Holocaust much more interesting than the comparison between you and Thomas Bernhard.

EJ. Seeing Austria critically connects Bernhard and me, but others do that too.

GH. The three of you are Austria's unholy trinity.

EJ. Yes, but I don't really belong there. I am the outsider, most definitely, among the three of us; [Handke and Bernhard] are perfectly sure of themselves and it's this self-assurance with which Bernhard writes, always in a spoken language, which I only use in my plays. With Bernhard you have the feeling it's written at a crazy speed as if he first dictated it and then wrote it down. It's always spoken.

GH. He loved to talk—

EJ. Oh yes, he could talk ten to twelve hours non-stop, people would beg him to finally stop—I know that, I know some of his friends—and Bernhard would say, "Well, then I'll top it off with the thirteenth hour." (*Laughs.*) The others were all already lying on the floor. I am not like that at all. I am the silent woman.

GH. But the three of you have written the Austria of the twentieth century.

EJ. Still, this dominant discourse of men is something a woman cannot do. She has to somehow sidle through subversively or find other ways . . . They will add my name now, probably because I got the Nobel Prize.

Otherwise, they wouldn't mention me in the same breath with Handke and Bernhard. I am absolutely sure. If I am sure of anything, this is it. A woman does not represent when she is talking, while a man does represent. It is speaking-to-all, while a woman, even if she speaks to others, probably always speaks to herself, into herself. And probably this "we" [that I tend to use], this "we" is always a camouflage for what one cannot say, because a woman doesn't have that "I," she has to construct herself.

GH. And a man?

EJ. They all stand behind him, the [male] academics; he stands in front and the others are behind him—a wall.

GH. Many people who know your work assume that you have a special connection to Derrida.

EJ. No, no, I read very little by him. But it is not my job to interpret, others can do that.

GH. I see your connection to Derrida via Heidegger.

EJ. Derrida is also a stranger, a foreigner. Jewish, oriental, French, African—

GH. —who then lives in Paris.

EJ. I have to say, I don't understand [his work]. It is all very difficult, very dark.

GH. Hmm, I still think you come together through Heidegger.

EJ. A lot comes together through Heidegger, Sartre, who even learned German to be able to read *Being and Time*, Simone de Beauvoir too, and Arendt. It's interesting that the women arrived at a rather political way

of philosophizing—Beauvoir, through her femi-
nism, *The Other Sex*; and Arendt with her political
thinking about totalitarianism. While abstraction,
pure thinking, remained with the men. Roland
Barthes in his *Mythologies* describes this with very
specific examples, such as the famous American
photo exhibition "The Family of Man."[9] It's been
quite some time since I read the *Mythologies*. But I did
use Barthes's *Michelet* in my most recent text [*The
Silent Maiden*], where he delineates how the historian
Michelet feminizes history, how he biologizes it, how
he compares history with old aunts, with sexless old
aunts or with menstruating women; it's pretty
unusual, after all, that a historian takes the human
body as a paradigm for historical processes. So, while
writing the play, *The Silent Maiden*, I couldn't resist
taking something from there (*laughs*).

GH. How do you use your sources?

EJ. It works like that: I have the book in front of me and
I thumb through it, and then it is a sort of lunging for
something that will be useful for the text, that'll move
the text forward, one bears down like a bird of prey,
one claws oneself in like a sea eagle, who catches his
fish, in flight so to speak, its claws barely touching the

9 "The Family of Man" was curated by Edward Steichen in 1955 at
the New York Museum of Modern Art. The photographs included in
the exhibition focussed on the people and cultures around the world
as an expression of humanism in the decade following World War II.
In *Mythologies* (1956), Barthes criticized the exhibition as being an
example of his concept of myth—the dramatization of an ideological
message.

water and then flies right up, or like the buzzard catches the mouse. So then I am—and that's a metaphor, which really fits me—a bird of prey that hacks out the stuff.

GH. The German term "Greifvogel"—a bird that uses its claws to catch and kill—illustrates the action much more accurately.

EJ. It really works like that, I hack my fish out of the water, as it were, and this could be a different fish in a different spot.

GH. That reminds me of Peter Brook who once said in one of his workshop demonstrations, he doesn't "invent" things, rather, he is a vulture who picks them up from everywhere.

EJ. Interesting that he also compares his work to that of a bird of prey. Though, the vulture isn't really a bird of prey. A vulture hacks his stuff out of a carcass, while I, in flight, so to speak, grab the living thing, the living, bleeding prey out of the water or the mouse, like the buzzard, out of the ground.

GH. Makes sense, as a director he works differently.

EJ. As a director he works on a text, so actually on dead matter, as a vulture, while I have to still create something.

But what's really important to me is that I am not an authority of secondary texts. I can't say I know Nietzsche so well that I know exactly what to look up, my knowledge is not concrete, it's rather a kind of *sample*, like the cloud, which is a storage space, from where you take things out later. Maybe my brain is such a cloud, where I search around out of a vague inkling and then I might find something completely different and I immediately know—that's it. At any rate, what I am after is language per se. Of course [my texts] are not collages; it's always only just one quote, which I frequently alter as well. So it's not exactly as in Heidegger, or only rarely, but rather like a marker on the way one is taking, and then one ties Ariadne's thread around it and continues with the thread, knowing one can return if necessary, in case one loses the way.

GH. Those are beautiful images.

EJ. Images—it's all I have, because I cannot think.

GH. Well, I am not going to write that . . . (*both laugh*)

EJ. There you go, I am telling you a profound truth and then you don't want to use it.

GH. How do you arrive at the sources you use? In *Charges* you weave Aeschylus's play about the fifty Danaid virgins fleeing from forced marriages and the myth of Io—who was turned into a shiny white cow by her lover Zeus to protect her from his jealous wife Hera, who in turn has her guarded by hundred-eyed Argos who in turn is killed on Hera's command, who then has Io chased by a gadfly from Europe to Asia.

EJ. I really can't say. Of course, I am thinking about what I could use to provide the rhythm for the text, so to speak.

GH. And that's already in your head or are you then reading a lot?

EJ. Well, I've got to have it in my head, I couldn't start reading all Greek plays.

GH. Does that go back to your high school education?

EJ. No, we did not have ancient Greek and we hardly dealt with Greek tragedies, Greek drama in school.

GH. So, then, how do you get to these sources. You just have them in your head?

EJ. No, otherwise I would not be a writer, I would be a theorist. I don't really have an academic education, I am an autodidact, I did study, but I did not finish— *Theaterwissenschaft* [Theater History / Theater Studies]—and you know what you learn there (*both laugh*). At least here, I am sure it's different where you are—

GH. No comment. —But you do read a lot, I assume.

EJ. I read a lot of mysteries.

GH. I know. But where—

EJ. Well, of course, once I decided to write *Totenauberg*, I read Arendt and Heidegger, but I read them from a different perspective than a philosopher who is trained to make completely different connections. I read them as literature and Heidegger himself was literary minded, he has written a lot about poetic language and he also penned awful poems, like Hegel (*laughs*). When philosophers produced poetry, it was terrible poetry. Yes, it's interesting to see who becomes a thinker and who processes all this in a poetic language.

GH. As translator, I have to do my homework. Because of you, I read a lot more of Heidegger, also in English.

EJ. But you really don't have to use the existing Heidegger translations. Or you can change the translations, after all, I change Heidegger too.

GH. Yes, but you come up with such terrific terms—

EJ. (*laughs*). But you do too. You've got them.

GH. So then, how do you finally decide on your "secondary" material?

EJ. I really can't answer that. Because it happens in a kind of in-between-zone of thinking, trying to grasp it with logical thinking would not work. When I send one of my texts to Bärbel Lücke for example, most recently it was The *Silent Maiden*, she has a thousand ideas and insights and associations; that's different, yes, because she has a more profound education than I and then, in the case of the NSU, she uses René Girard for her interpretation.[10] I have also used him before, for *Rechnitz*, but he would have been wrong for *The Silent Maiden*, because I made it an allegory and that would have been a doubling, I would say once again what's said in the play, so then, it has to be something that works against the text, which I can sink my teeth in. But those things occur in an in-between zone.

---

10 Barbel Lücke is a German author and literary critic. She has written extensively about Jelinek's linguistic deconstructions.

GH. Sometimes that happens with translating.

EJ. Sure, you also work with associations.

GH. Yes, those are fun and you encourage me to go way over the top with them and I do, in the first draft. But in the next drafts of texts such as *Rechnitz* and *Charges* and your great novel *The Children of the Dead,* which are culturally so specific and linguistically so precise— you don't ever cheat, no matter how far out you drive your associations—I am eventually taken back to the text by your rhythm and logic and syntax, almost automatically, albeit via some detours.

EJ. Yes, you can trigger such linguistic associations as you work with them in English, you can trigger them and once that happens, they keep coming, also in English.

GH. But the other language also can take you in a completely different direction.

EJ. Sure, but English has a tradition of punning, of silly word games, while in the German theater culture I get constantly beaten over the head by the critics for mine. But I think using language as such to tell the truth, even against its will, is a literary tradition. If it's granted to Arno Schmidt, to James Joyce—they can grant it to me too. It is an acknowledged [literary tool] even in German-language cultures as in the case of Arno Schmidt and his punning was much more outrageous than mine.

GH. In *Charges* there is a term, which of course plays a big part: *Einbürgerung*, which translates idiomatically into naturalization—

EJ. Yeah and that's absurd, because naturalization—it's also used in German, "he is a naturalized German"—but that's the opposite of *Ein-bürgerung*, which is an over-acculturation, to squeeze someone into a nation, while the other is a natural condition.

GH. Yes, but when you take American culture at large, there is nothing "natural," everything has to be artificially "improved," your skin, your hair, your breasts, your eyelids so that it looks "natural." In Arizona, where I live, you can get a facelift at any shopping mall.

EJ. NOOH!

GH. Food is processed to make it taste better than natural.

EJ. You are ahead of us there.

GH. Now you push the term *Einbürgerung* further and further. You also would have pushed "naturalization" way over the top, had you used that term. But you are not using it, so *Einbürgerung* pops up in different contexts with different meanings, based on the prefix *ein-*, which connotes both the number one and the action of infusing something into something else and even "preserving" as in preserving fruit (*einmachen*). So crassly literal, *"Ein–bürgerung"* translates into "infusing citizenship." Now citizenship needs a verb to suggest the act of obtaining it, which would break your rhythm. It's not a very flexible term, at best "ship" could be connected to the "boat" of the refugees. But they are nowhere near their respective places in your text where I could spin a chain of wordplays which will take me back to the point you are ultimately making. And those points are astutely targeted.

EJ. Well, you are also such a processed citizen (*laughs*). Now you are finally naturalized, away from Vienna, stuffed into your nature—the true one!

GH. Hmm, I have to think about that. We were on the subject of untranslatable terms. We talked about Celan before. Now, the correspondence between Heidegger and Celan has just been published and was discussed in the media this week. There is the word *Andenken*, which you love too. It usually connotes memory, it also means souvenir, but that doesn't play into what I am getting at. In the case of Celan and Heidegger the issue of course is the different meaning of memory for the Jewish poet and for the philosopher as an early, [at least publicly] unrepenting admirer of Hitler. Now Heidegger teases out the verb in the noun *An-denken*, which suggests the mental process of approaching a subject, a "thinking toward." You also introduce the term in that sense as a starting point for further transformations of meanings.

EJ. Yes, thinking-toward, sure, some things will work in translation, some just won't, then you just have to make up for it in some other place, where the English term may trigger a wordplay, but not its German equivalent.

GH. Well, yes, it seems quite logical talking about it, but in actuality, once you start playing, the word stays in the game, so to speak, and for a long period of time. And each time with a different, context-depending connotation. So what do I do then, in case I ignored it before? The sentences won't make any sense, because the meaning emerges strictly out of the chain of mutating words.

EJ. Hmm. When you take language by its word and then "twist it around in the mouth," as we say here, that is when it starts getting interesting.

GH. That is how the picture emerges.

EJ. First the word, that's already different than the figurative meaning and then turning it all around.

GH. And even if I manage to find only one equivalent pun in translation, it just sits there, for no obvious reason, let alone necessity, but it continues—

EJ. No, it's not simply about one wordplay. It always serves some message, whatever it may be.

GH. And your playing with certain terms, idioms, quotations weaves through the entire text, sometimes getting entangled in utter nonsense, which turns out to actually be the point of your take on a given situation and the "true picture" emerges only once the tapestry is completed. And your linguistic strategies are so precise, so tightly intertwined—the translator has to pay the closest attention not to drop a stitch.

EJ. That's because of my training in music; my treatment of language is compositional. As we discussed earlier, I have studied composition. I can sense when something isn't right, rhythmically. Sometimes I can't say why, but I know there's a snag, it just isn't working, I notice right away, that's something that's been drilled into me since earliest childhood, I have learned that from scratch. Basically, it is a compositional process, I often said that, but I haven't talked about it in ages.

GH. That's how it works for me in translation as well. A sentence may be grammatically correct, but something's still wrong about it. The Dutch director Johan Simons, who is now rehearsing *The Silent Maiden* at the Munich Kammerspiele, who has staged several of your plays, said that he approaches your texts through music, through the body.

EJ. That's because he doesn't know German very well, there must be another level where he understands me, maybe as I understand Derrida or Heidegger on another level of cognition.

GH. It's somewhat ironical that Derrida died the year you received the Nobel Prize.

EJ. Yes, it's crazy. They say he had hoped to get it.

GH. Oh yes.

EJ. I hope it wasn't disappointment (*laughs*) he died from because I got it. That would be terrible. But it really is a little spooky.

GH. Considering his way of writing, I think he'd have wanted nothing more than transforming his thinking into a *Dichtung*, a poetic work, a work of literature.

EJ. I often hear about the profoundest thinkers—whom I can't follow at all, not even their simplest sentences—that they actually just wanted to be artists. Their great ideal—but for that you really don't have to know anything.

GH. Well—

EJ. Writing functions on a different cognitive level. You have to leave yourself behind yourself, even if you are talking about yourself and throw yourself into something else, which is the music of language. And since I am able to concentrate extremely well and have this compulsion to associate, this obsessive twisting and turning of language to tap it for another meaning, that goes so far that I sometimes read a completely different word from what's written, and then I see it is different, it just sounds similar.

GH. You have a moment like that in *Charges*, when the refugees try to read the brochure and instead of "unprejudiced," they first read "unperjured."

EJ. Yes, yes, that brochure was a real treasure trove, of course.

GH. It really exists?

EJ. It sure does. You couldn't even make that up! I got it from the web.[11] That's what people receive who apply for citizenship, meaning refugees who have no status. They have to read this, apparently it's been written by a lawyer, a law professor, it's totally insane. Now that opens all connections to free-associating.

GH. That brings me to a choice of wordplay I want to double check with you. The speakers are the refugees,

---

11 *Zusammenleben in Österreich* [Coexistence in Austria], the brochure published by the Integration Centre, Interior Ministry of Austria in 2013–14. Available at: http://goo.gl/gGP7al (last accessed on April 26, 2016).

imitating the mindset and the voices of the local people, who think that asylum seekers need to be reined in [*eingezäumt*]—in German, the term relates to horses, which takes you to fenced in [*eingezäunt*] by just changing one letter from "m" to "n". So you play with *"einzäumen"* that suggests reins and *"einzäunen"* [to fence in] which leads you to refugees must be tamed *"gezähmt"* like savages.

I start with "to be barred from" which gets me to bars as a misunderstanding, but I lose the taming "like savages." So, since you weave in allusions to Catholicism and Islam [the latter more or less veiled—pun not intended here] I can sneak in a [silly] allusion to the religious prohibition of drinking. You say: *Menschen wie wir gehören eingezäumt, nein, eingezäunt, Entschuldigung, gezähmt gehören wir Wilden, damit wir Sie nicht überschwemmen . . .* [Folks like us must be barred, put in bars, no, behind them (we don't drink), fenced in like savages, so that we won't flood you, no, no, that must not be . . .]

It seems a small matter, but still, I am moving far away from your images here, so I thought, I should put my additions in parentheses—in this case "we don't drink"—so it is clear that they are not in your text.

EJ. You don't have to use parentheses. Those are your creative contribution, your linguistically creative contributions. And sometimes it takes you to a completely different place simply because it is already embedded in the text. Translating really is a fascinating process. *Über-setzen*—crossing by boat.

GH. The refugees . . . Wow . . . There are other kinds of insertions into *Charges* I want to run by you. You refer to well-known people without mentioning their names. For example the Russian soprano—I love the resonance of Tony here,[12] but of course, you are talking of Anna Netrebko. You also talk about "the thinker," who is Heidegger. I felt I needed to give the reader–audience some cue. I thought that people often don't recall names instantly, which lends itself to the oldest shtick routines of trying to remember, so Netrebko took me to neb—nebbish.

EJ. Exactly, that's wonderful. But she certainly is also known in the US.

GH. Yes, but you never mention her name, or Heidegger's.

EJ. Of course I am quite aware that I am a provincial author. Since I do not travel, I claw myself into what happens here. Yes, Heidegger "Why do I stay in the provinces?" that's also by Heidegger—why didn't he accept the call to Berlin, why did he stay in Freiburg, so there is a certain kinship here. Well, and then there was Hannah Arendt, when she came back. He would have wanted to seamlessly resume their relationship. So now she was the American Jewish woman, so to speak, and what is the Jews' special expertise? Money. And immediately he gave her the task of auctioning

12 Refers to Tony Soprano, the protagonist of the internationally popular TV series *The Sopranos* (1999–2007).

his *Being and Time*, so that he can get money. That was, that is, I mean that is an anti-Semitism that was so deeply rooted in the Germans that they weren't even conscious of it. But since I come from a Jewish family, I was very much made aware of it since earliest childhood.

GH. Provincial, especially for our generation in the wake of the Nazi's "blood and soil" glorification, has a very negative association—"country bumpkin" versus "the urbane".

EJ. Yes, that's exactly what happened to me. When I got the award, everyone said, of course, "she calls herself provincial." What I never meant as a negative, but used in order to explain my horizon, was used against me to brand me as a "provincial cow," though I have always lived in Vienna, and Vienna is a cosmopolitan city, a small one, relatively, but one of the cultural capitals. So they can't say I come from the provinces. Maybe they think I am from Styria, because I was born there, but that was just the family's country place and my parents happened to be there when I was born.

GH. I am very interested in the perception of "provincial" in postcolonialist discourse. The Indian historian Dipesh Chakrabarty's influential book *Provincializing Europe* was very important to my understanding of the notion of "where we come from."

EJ. I would be very interested in that.

GH. It s not about "provincialism" in the sense we are talking about here, but rather about the postcolonial world's continued generalizing perception of Europe as one cultural–hegemonic power. Instead it should also be seen as broken down into regions, provinces. Chakrabarty then discusses India's history from a Heideggerian and Marxian perspective as a precarious balance between place, origin, tradition on the one hand and contemporary social challenges on the other. It seems to me that this dialectic also defines the "provincialism" of your literary themes.

EJ. I think, one either penetrates a very small space very deeply or remains on the surface and enters big spaces.

GH. But isn't it precisely that depth that makes it universal?

EJ. Yes, but the universal is not the place. Because in my novels, for example—my plays, at least in that sense are abstract—the province is really present, Styria, where I actually spent all vacations, the Styrian woods, all that was the uncanny to me. *The Children of the Dead* take place in Styria. [Austria's] history culminates in the provinces. And that goes back to some extent to early childhood experiences. Because I have come to Styria since I was a baby. To condense it, literary speaking [*um es zu verdichten*] it has to be brought home. That's what's so un*heim*lich [uncanny] about *Heim*at. The word *Heim*—"home," features in both.

GH. Now we have entered Freudian territory. I usually try to avoid Freud when I am talking about your work, especially to you, so you won't think, 'now she uses the most obvious cliché,' I mean, with regard to your staging of familial relationships.

EJ. Well, I did read Freud. He was of course a magnificent writer. And I quoted him in several plays, again and again, where he fits in—or doesn't fit in, sometimes I consciously denied myself the opportunity—because it was too obvious, as I [denied][13] myself René Girard in the NSU play.

　　—Aha, there we have it—*vergreifen-verkneifen* and *vergreifen*. A typical slip of tongue, which could happen to anyone, but it's absolutely typical for me.

GH. I really had to laugh about the term *"verkniffen."* It sounds so funny hearing it with an "Americanized ear" so to speak, and I haven't heard this word since my childhood.

EJ. Yes, those are childhood words, the Austrian language we speak, you at any rate, you conserved it like in a time capsule, while I continued to speak it. But young people don't understand it, because language gets depleted. That beautiful old Viennese my father spoke, and those idioms! "Strain yourself through the sewer cover," (*sich im Kanaldeckel passieren*) things like that. He was half Jewish and therefore able to survive

---

13 Here Jelinek intended to say, "denied," a repetition of the previously used, somewhat quirky German term for "denying oneself something" [*sich etwas verkneifen*]. Instead she says *"vergreifen"* which usually connotes a sexual assault.

the holocaust in Vienna as a forced laborer of sorts, a chemist at Siemens, during the Nazi time, when all the new bosses were German, so everyone had to sing "We are sailing against England—ahoy!" and instead of "ahoy" my father always used to sing *"amoy,"* Viennese dialect for *einmal*, some time, whenever, meaning never, as in "[Elfriede], you are going to America!"— "Yeah, whenever." *Ahoy–Amoy*. Exactly the opposite. Don't you know it?

GH. I had to hear you say it a few times until I heard the subtext.

EJ. Exactly. And that's what he sang out loud. In his precarious position, it was a pretty subversive act. I would certainly not have dared to do that. And that language—that's truly absurd—that language can say "some time", when it means "never."

GH. You do that all the time.

EJ. Yes, exactly. Maybe I've really got it since early childhood, from my father and my aunts, his two sisters, who always praised me for my little language jokes, maybe that's what triggered it in me. "Ahoy-amoy" that's genius, really!

GH. Yes, and you keep repeating it and I am desperate! *"Macht nichts,"* for example. means, depending on the tone of voice, "it doesn't matter" or "don't do anything." And there are a few other such seemingly innocuous idioms. So, it all goes back to your family's dinner conversations!

EJ. Yes, yes. And the praise. When children can show off and everybody laughs about the funny things they say, they'll get more and more into it, because every child will try to go even further, if she gets rewarded or admired for it, that's normal. "Ego gratification" an old school friend of mine told me; she is a psychoanalyst in the Californian prison system.

GH. So, there are the Freudian slips, the father's survivor's humor and Heidegger's digging up of word roots—

EJ. Oh yes—*"Das Nichts nichtet,"* that's a play on words.

GH. Sure! "The Nothing noths," as I read in one of the Heidegger translations. If I used that in any of your texts, it would just be a bad translation.

EJ. Yeah, but in context it will become clear that it is not, because if it were, everything would be badly translated, but in context you can see how it develops and where it comes from and how in the end it all makes sense.

GH. And then there is the reference to the nameless "thinker" in *Charges* who probably is easier to recognize in the original German, than in translation. So I tried to sneak in a couple of cues, which I ran by you via email: Heidegg-whatever, Heidegghead, Heideggman.

EJ. Yes, those are the huge questions of our times! (*Laughs.*)

GH. Well, that's the problem—when do I get too cute, too silly, too "funny"?

EJ. Okay, you can't ever be funny enough!

GH. Okay—

EJ. Don't be shy!

GH. That's a really important point.

EJ. No, don't ever hold back, that is the first commandment. I tell all my directors—by now most of them don't have to be told anymore—it must be comical, that's what's most important. So, if you have two solutions, you always must take the comical one.

Even if it's perhaps not as good as the other one, but it must be used—it's a stylistic tool, it's not satire, it's a tool of mockery: Language that grins about itself, so, actually, it is a bitter, mocking laugh.

GH. But at other times you can be quite endearingly funny. For example, when you insert yourself in the text, such as in connection with a quote: "I'll have to look that up myself."

EJ. Yes, that was true. I still had to look something up about the virgin, but the book hadn't yet been delivered, it came the afternoon after I had written this.

GH. And this time I even dared to insert myself as the translator—

EJ. Of course, after all, you are me in that sense.

GH. So, when you write: "I have to write," I add "And I have to translate!"

EJ. Yes, exactly, you are I.

GH. And then your *"Zug"* [train] kept me busy. In German you can do a lot with this term. There's "train of refugees"—I first used "column," because the picture of all the refugees on foot seemed clearer—but then the meaning mutates into *Zug* for "draught," Zug, the town in Switzerland, etc. In the end, since *Zug* sounds funny when pronounced in English, I played with the German word as well.

Perhaps the most problematic term to translate is the German, *"man"* as in "one does that." Commonly used in German, it instantly comes across as "un-English." It's a big problem in *Charges*, since it indicates the speaker's de-individualized perception of refugees and how the refugees eventually see themselves.

EJ. Yes, one is "we," the other is "you" in English.

GH. Or "they." So the editor asks, "who are the 'they'," which relates to my earlier question "who are the 'we'." It gets more tricky because of Heidegger haunting your language; and Heidegger's definition of *"man"* as the *"uneigentliche Mensch,"* or the "inauthentic man," in Heideggerian terminology. Therefore, losing the "one" in English or not being as consistent with it as you can be in German, "one" loses an essential psychological aspect in the play. And the question is: where to preserve the foreignness of the text. Generally, it is expected that one shouldn't notice that it is a translated text.

EJ. What doesn't fit in must be made to fit in.

GH. It gets naturalized! I wonder whether it reveals an attitude towards anything foreign. At the risk of generalization, "one" versus "they" might reflect the notion of American individualism versus a German emphasis on "one's" responsibilities towards society as a whole.

In any event, I thought that the "one" problem can only be solved dramaturgically, in performance. It depends on the director and the ensemble's understanding of social responsibility. They have to find the right balance in rehearsal. Those are really challenging questions for a theater company.

EJ. You already had the experience with the New York production of *Jackie*. Although it still is relatively simple there, because it is a real monologue and it's clear who is talking. One would have to see how that works in a more abstract text, such as *Rechnitz*.

GH. But the really good directors have filled what you call "linguistic templates" very excitingly, even psychologically in a non-naturalistic way as Jossi Wieler's work, or, like Nicolas, who found his own associative stage language, which is the theatrical equivalent of your linguistic strategies.

EJ. Nicolas adds more voices, because he is also a musician. That's what's important. And then he adds his improvisations, they are incredibly comical, but he knows what he can add.

GH. And you have Johan Simons, the artistic director of the Munich Kammerspiele until the end of the 2014–15 season, who staged the premiere productions of your *Winterreise*, and *The City. The Street. The Attack* about Maximilian Strasse—Munich's exclusive shopping street—the murder of the famous fashion designer Rudolph Moshammer, and the brutal search of your home by the Bavarian police. As we speak, Simons is rehearsing *The Silent Maiden*. And of course there is Jossi Wieler, the defining director, most recently, of *Rechnitz*.

EJ. Unfortunately, Jossi has no longer the time to direct plays since he took over the Stuttgart Opera. He is very precise and he distills characters from my linguistic templates. Not psychologically, but on another level. Terrific. I work with a hammer, Jossi with tweezers and awl, to pull out the fishbones, so to speak—

GH. —which become absolutely real human beings.

EJ. It's amazing that he can do that. It is something the others can't.

GH. It just shows that the way you talk about linguistic templates is somewhat misleading. Your texts are multilayered, they can be processed in many ways.

EJ. Yes. Directors can take what parts they want to work on. I offer them the whole thing. One takes this, the other that. It's possible to make many plays out of a single one.

GH. How do you react to directors who cut as much as two-thirds of your plays?

EJ. I am always very thankful. I always worry that the audience will begin to get bored, and that would be terrible. But I also want my plays to exist as [complete] texts and that they get read, but that hasn't happened. Because for a reading audience those are still plays, and plays are hardly read by the general reading audience. But my plays are texts, basically like the novels, just that the ones are texts for speaking, the others for reading. And that's the only difference. The methods are the same.

GH. You said earlier that you revise a lot, that is, while writing. But not anymore when the texts go into production.

EJ. Yes, I rewrite several times. That leads to more associations. In the second version one can be much freer with them. What was just an allusion in the first one, can become too rich in the second version, it happens, it can get overloaded, I tend to do that, I try to rein myself in (*laughs*) but then it gets more and more and each time more targeted because there's already something to work with.

GH. It's similar with translating. One gets more daring the second time around.

EJ. Yes, yes, then one can see where it goes, where it works and where it can sustain some more and where it gets too much again. I always tend toward the too much, all editors know that, I mean Nils [Tabert, the editor of Rowohlt Theater division] cut 30 pages of *The Silent Maiden*, that's cutting thirty of 240 manuscript pages.

GH. *Charges* by comparison is a very compact play, 58 pages in your manuscript.

EJ. It was a rush job.

GH. How long do you work on a performance text?

EJ. That varies quite a bit. As I said, on *Charges* no longer than two to three weeks. *The Silent Maiden* took the longest ever, six months with interruptions.

GH. It is interesting that since you received the Nobel Prize you have written primarily texts for the theater and brief prose texts—

EJ. Yes, and funny enough, I received the Nobel specifically for a play, which has rarely been performed and it was the final push so to speak.[14] Christoph Marthaler directed it. I heard in an interview, that the Nobel committee made a special trip to Zürich to see the production, since Kjell Espmark, the chair of the committee always thought that my plays are undramatic, they are not plays. So they all flew to Zürich, they didn't go to Munich where it premiered, they wanted to be incognito, it's all very secret. And afterwards Espmark said, it was one of the most powerful theatrical experiences in his life. He would have never imagined that such texts could function on stage. So, actually, I got the award as a dramatist. Well, it was the final impetus.

GH. Why are you writing so many texts for the theater now?

EJ. As a substitute for living probably, because I always let others speak for me in other places, since I can't

---

14 *In den Alpen* [In the Alps] premiered at the Munich Kammerspiele in association with the Zürich Schauspielhaus in 2002.

go there myself. I haven't seen productions of my plays in the theater in many years—only on DVDs. So it is an ersatz life so to speak.

GH. But you've always been politically active. Intervention was always important to you and you do intervene—

EJ. Yeah, it would be nice if I could believe that one can really intervene, I am trying, but I don't have the feeling that it effects anything, especially in Austria where people are extremely negative towards me. Maybe not so much so after the Nobel, critics have become more cautious, but you just have to read the posts against me—

GH. Well, you disturb and that's an important task of the theater. I often wonder how you can deal with the issues you confront, such as the case of Josef Fritzl, who kept his daughter locked up for years in his basement and fathered her children or the NSU murders—

EJ. Fritzl and the murder of the baby, his daughter gave birth to twins and he flung one of them into the fire, infanticide, that this man could kill his own child— well, it was already dead, but I certainly wouldn't put this beyond him. The Nazis used to do that, they threw babies against the wall or—they did everything one couldn't even imagine.

GH. How can you live in this world?

EJ. I can't, I can't anyway. I am ill, after all.

GH. But it takes incredible courage.

EJ. Well, I don't know. But one processes these things as a text, a play. Sure, it takes you in—but maybe I would be better off if I weren't writing such things. I have no idea. I don't want to blame [my interests for my condition]. But I have been asked a few times, by my publishers: how can you expose yourself to all that, no wonder you are not well (*laughs*). I don't want to make this connection [between my work and my condition], but it is strange, I always have to instantly rip out things that are buried, in the cellar or in the ground as in *Rechnitz*.

GH. I think your body of work is the strongest testimony of the times we live in.

EJ. Yes, but I don't offer anything positive, one should see that too, but it doesn't interest me, I am only interested in things I need to work through, but not in anything positive, unlike Yasmina Reza, who actually does see the abyss in the idyll, but her plays are still comedies. That's a completely different kind of theater, masterly, of course, but different. Or Allen Ayckbourne's comedies, they are terrific, and Woody Allen's films, they are certainly great and evil is already in them too, but—still, my work always turns comical too, if that weren't possible, I probably wouldn't do it. Especially, the NSU piece.

GH. Sometimes it takes very careful reading to discover the comedy in your intricate wordplays.

EJ. And it takes directors who know how to direct that. Nicolas pushes it further into the comical, grotesque.

Jossi [Wieler] takes it more seriously and stays closer inside the text, that's different again.

GH. When people ask me about the absence of hope in your writing, I tell them that the hope is in the fact that you keep writing about matters that need to be confronted and worked through. That literature and theater can still do that.

EJ. Well, and then I have Oscar Wilde to recuperate [from my plays]. That happens when I translate Eugène Labiche, Georges Feydeau, and Wilde.

GH. Last, but not least, you are also a translator.

EJ. I translate only comedies.

GH. Do you pick the plays or are those assignments?

EJ. Those are assignments, first by my former publisher, [Bansemer & Nyssen] also by directors.

GH. And how was your knack for that kind of comedy discovered? Did you express your interest?

EJ. No, no, it was the publishers. The copyright had just expired, so they asked me if I'd be interested in translating Labiche. And I was, those plays are brilliant.

GH. You also translated Thomas Pynchon's *Gravity's Rainbow* [*Das Enden der Parabel*] in 1981, your first major translation project.

EJ. That was pure hubris, because of course I was not able to do that, but I just did it. One has to be totally solid in the target language, but one also has to have a real sense for the source language, such as you for mine—and since I know you, I know with absolute certainty, that only a native speaker of German, that is of Austrian German can really translate me. No one else. I learned this through you. It was clear to me earlier, but in you I found the embodiment, you grew up exactly as I did, you are almost the same age, you experienced the same things and then, at age 20 or so, you threw yourself into a totally different language, which you probably know better than your mother tongue, because your vocabulary expanded and still you preserved your sense for the mother tongue. Well, in my case that's the only way it works. It's different with other authors, I am sure that it's not a problem with them. But with me it doesn't work in any other way. That's just the way it is.

GH. I think I had the advantage that both my daughters were born and grew up in the States. I was pregnant with my first daughter when I moved there. So we practically arrived at the same time. I had 10 years of English in school and I always loved the language. So I thought that with the birth of my daughter I could also absorb English as the language of childhood. I think it is very important for a translator to experience the language of childhood in both languages.

EJ. Do your daughters speak German?

GH. No.

EJ. Funny, I never asked you this. It just occurs to me now.

GH. It was an act of rebellion in a way against the language of guilt, as I perceived it then. It was embarrassing to speak German in the 1960s.

EJ. Yes, I am convinced it was a question of guilt.

GH. I remember a column in *The New York Times* by Peter Schneider, the German writer who lived in New York for a while during the 80s. He wrote that if your child ran into the street you'd be embarrassed to shout "*Halt!*" That's so true.

EJ. Oh! Is it still that way?

GH. No, it has changed.

EJ. Since Germany's soccer World Cup victory this summer Germany finally is innocent.

GH. Have you been watching the games?

EJ. Only the final matches.

GH. This time I watched every single game for "cultural studies," so to speak.

EJ. It's not easy. But I think baseball is a lot more difficult. I made a terrible fool of myself in my Pynchon translation. There was a baseball expression, which I had not recognized as such and it was pointed out to me rather unkindly that it was stupid.

GH. It seems to me you put yourself down a bit much with regard to Pynchon. After all, you introduced him to German readers.

EJ. Well, let's say I have my merits, but when I worked on it, I didn't know what I was doing. In the end I realized that I did not see the difficulties. I had wonderful helpers, there was an American friend, he had the same cultural background as Pynchon and like him he was interested in the soldiers' songs of World War II, so he could explain them to me. Then, there was a member of the OSS [Office of Strategic Services], he was Jewish and served once in the US Intelligence Service. I didn't know the names of the individual parts of a gun. He was my expert in weapon technology. He explained to me how a revolver works.

GH. How do you always find these people?

EJ. I found the OSS agent in the Austrian Communist Party. (*Laughs.*) The Americans had even sentenced him to death for espionage for the Soviet Union. He was eventually released. He was a valuable resource for my translation. He is dead now.

GH. What were your mistakes?

EJ. Countless, simply because I don't know American culture well enough. As we have said before, translating isn't only language—you have to live in that culture. Luckily, *Gravity's Rainbow* does not take place in America. It's about American GIs, but it is set in the Zone, in occupied post–World War II Germany, and in the Nazi period, and there is a lot of German stuff—otherwise I would have been lost. I could have never translated his later works, say *Mason & Dixon*.

GH. But your translation of *Gravity's Rainbow* is still the most current translation.

EJ. Well, my friend helped me with the translation and I had asked Thomas Piltz to revise it. Otherwise I'd have been up the creek. But it really was a killer. I literally worked a couple of years four hours every morning, four hours in the afternoon—every single day.

GH. Yeah, tell me about it! You also translated Marlowe's *The Jew of Malta* for Peter Zadek's 2001 production at the Vienna Burgtheater.

EJ. Yes. I had just finished my first so-called secondary play to [Gotthold Ephraim] Lessing's *Nathan the Wise*, which is always performed as this peace vision (between Jews, Arabs and the Knights of the Temple, set in Jerusalem) and I responded by showing the insanity in the Middle East between Palestinians and Israel. And Peter Zadek wanted to show this as well in his production of *The Jew of Malta*. So he asked me to translate the play.

GH. Can you explain your concept of "secondary play."

EJ. This idea came to me like a flash. I don't know, it was a real inspiration. I thought why shouldn't it be possible to write continuations of plays. They could be either short continuations or dialectical juxtapositions. I had done this with *Nathan the Wise*. The fact that Zadek then asked me to translate *The Jew of Malta* rather than his wife, Elizabeth Plessen, who is an excellent translator, seemed like an indication that he had something specific in mind. I don't know. Maybe it was because he had staged it in Vienna. It was a magnificent production, which, unfortunately, never got the attention it deserved.

GH. Marvin Carlson, a distinguished American scholar and critic questioned the production together with Zadek's brilliant staging of *The Merchant of Venice* [in Plessen's translation, 1988] in the contemporary Venetian banking world because of suspected traces of anti-semitism. [Zadek is Jewish.] Carlson's misreading of the director's dialectical dramaturgy is a perfect example of the problems of cultural translation. Perhaps in an effort to soften the shock for American audiences about a headline published in Theater Heute, in July 1990: *"Ich möchte lieber Verbrecher als Opfer sein"* (I'd rather be a perpetrator than a victim)—quoting Zadek from the magazine's interview with Zadek about his interpretation of Shylock—Carlson mistranslates the director's statement as quoted in the headline, replacing the term "perpetrator" with "rebel" so that it reads "I'd rather be a rebel than a victim."[15]

EJ. It leaves a trail of facts behind, doesn't it? The Israeli are the people who were the victim and never want to be victim again, they rather makes others the victims than becoming victims again. Psychoanalytically, this is completely understandable. It is horrible, but it is understandable.

15 See Gitta Honegger, "Lost in Translation," *The Routledge Companion to Dramaturgy* (Magda Romanska ed.) (Oxon, New York: Routledge, 2015), pp. 282–7.

GH. Yes, and that was completely misunderstood. And Zadek of course is as uncompromising as you and incredibly smart.

EJ. Yes, yes, we understood each other completely. We were in full agreement. I really prepared thoroughly. I used to think only in blank verse those days and I think, I even was speaking it. My play *Ulrike Maria* is also written in blank verse.[16] But only a few people noticed it. Which is a sign that it's right.

GH. Actually, the play you just finished, *The Silent Maiden*, about Beate Zschäppe the surviving leader of the National Socialist Underground, brings post–World War II terrorism in Germany to full circle: from *Ulrike Maria Stuart* about the Baader-Meinhof group's Red Army Fraction of the 1970s that started out as a rebellion against the legacy of Germany's Nazi past to the contemporary Neo-Nazis' deadly attacks on members of minority groups, with *Charges*, a powerful lament over the plight of refugees, to Aeschylus and Greek mythologies. What's next?

EJ. Vacation! I'll spend it in my backyard reading crime fiction.

---

16 Refers to Ulrike Meinhof, Gudrun Ensslin and Andreas Baader, based on Friedrich Schiller's verse play *Maria Stuart* (1800).